ELDERWRITERS:
CELEBRATE YOUR LIFE

SUE BAROCAS

ELDERWRITERS:
CELEBRATE YOUR LIFE

A Guide for Creating Your Own
Personal Legacy Document

SUE BAROCAS

ISBN-13: 978-1484825648
ISBN-10: 1484825640

Memories of You Before You Were Born used with permission of Wesley Kobylak.

Cover art created by Zachary Barocas.

This book is available for sale on amazon.com.

All writing examples are used with permission.

Publication date: 05/10/2013

In loving memory of my parents,
C. HOWARD AND MARCIA B. SHAFFER.

ACKNOWLEDGMENTS

MANY THANKS—

> » to all the Elderwriters participants for their ideas, enthusiasm, and support. I am especially grateful to those who contributed their writings for this guide. Some chose to be identified with their pieces and have been acknowledged in the text. Others preferred to remain anonymous. I regret I wasn't able to use all the contributions.

> » to Nina Alvarez, my editor, whose expertise and guidance were indispensable.

> » to my friends and family for their patience and support.

> » to Zach Barocas and Kimberley Yurkiewicz and Barb and Rollie Littlewood, whose assistance went way above and beyond the call of duty.

CONTENTS

PREFACE

Several years into my retirement, I decided to reactivate a long-standing interest in creative writing, with the idea of putting together a collection of short pieces to leave my sons—a set of verbal snapshots of the inner me. It turned out to be the most creative, introspective, and rewarding project I'd tackled in years. With the aid of the computer and Staples office supplies, I prepared a handsome document for each of my boys. I'm proud of my work.

I began to think about developing a continuing education course that would allow others to try their hand at a new style of memoir writing. Thus *Elderwriters: Celebrate Your Life!* was born. I teach the course through OASIS, a national continuing education organization with a program in Rochester, New York.

This guide is based on the Elderwriters course. It is designed for the individual writer. There is nothing in the approach that requires or anticipates writing skills beyond those learned in high school. The guide is focused on the specific goal of helping you create your own personal legacy document. Although there is considerable variation, Elderwriters personal legacy collections average twenty to twenty-five pages.

Is there something you'd like to say? Get to it. Personal legacy writing is energizing, engaging, enriching, and inexpensive. Elderwriters is for the writer in all of us!

Sue Barocas
www.elderwriters.com

How to Use this Book

MY GOALS FOR THIS BOOK ARE:

    a. to expand the options for personal legacy writing beyond the traditional memoir and autobiography.

    b. to provide motivation, encouragement, and support for that writing.

This book is a guide for creating your own personal legacy document (PLD). It is written as if you were going to work with me week by week. The chapters are sequenced to take you from the beginning stages of personal legacy writing through the printing and preserving of your document. If you follow the prompts and complete the exercises, you will have your own PLD by the end of Chapter 13. Presenting the material as a curriculum not only makes the process more manageable for the individual, but also provides an easy transition for those who wish to facilitate a class or small group.

Four themes are woven together in this guide: writing format, content, document construction, and helpful hints for the writer. These major themes are identified by the use of icons.

> **Writing Format**—the structure of the piece you are writing— list, short memoir, poem
>
> **Content**—the subject matter of the piece
>
> **Document Construction**—the components of your PLD, organization and layout, printing, preserving, and binding
>
> Help is on the way! **Helpful Hints** to enhance your writing process

Most chapters contain material from at least three of the themes.

We also have:

> Writing Exercises—A word about the writing exercises: there's nothing sacred about the exercises. Feel free to modify them, ignore them, add your own. You don't have to do anything you don't want to do. You're the boss.
>
> For easy access, I have made a list of the writing exercises for you in Appendix C.

Keep in mind that this is a write-as-you-go guide. I want you to be able to get started right away. Focus on working chapter by chapter. Don't worry about how far you have to go. Take it a step at a time. Get into it.

WITH, OR WITHOUT, COLLEAGUES

We don't all approach new tasks the same way. A good way to use this guide is with other people—a small group: a couple of friends, your book discussion group, members of your church or synagogue. Find a meeting place, set up a schedule—you're good to go. The group will fill in the gaps, consider your questions, make suggestions, clarify issues, spur you on, cheer with you, and dry your tears. And you will have the privilege of doing the same for them.

> The camaraderie and support of a group are often critical for motivation and success. For this reason, I have included an Introduction to Writing Groups in Appendix A.

Prefer to work alone? That's okay, too. Either way, I encourage you to read all the chapters. Topics that do not at first seem relevant may surprise you. The other thing that may surprise you is how much better and more comfortable you become with writing as time goes on. Writing and remembering turn out to be good companions. The words come. You just have to write them down.

You will need some supplies—here's the camp list:

» Post-its for flagging pages
» A highlighter
» Pens, pencils, and paper
» A few manila folders
» A dictionary and/or a thesaurus
» Enthusiasm

Keep your Post-its and highlighter handy. They help reduce information overload and make it easier to revisit paragraphs and ideas that caught your eye.

I'm ready if you are. Let's Celebrate Your Life!

CHAPTER I

WELCOME TO ELDERWRITERS CREATIVE LEGACY WRITING!

> ### IN CHAPTER I YOU WILL:
>
> » learn what a personal legacy document (PLD) is and what it is not
>
> » get answers to the question *Why create a personal legacy document?*
>
> » be introduced to the Elderwriters approach to personal legacy writing
>
> » begin to create your own PLD

WELCOME TO CREATIVE PERSONAL LEGACY WRITING

UNTIL NOW, PERSONAL LEGACY WRITING has been limited to the autobiography, the memoir, and, occasionally, the ethical will. Relatively few people leave behind one of these literary forms. Treasured family stories, fond memories, and personal wisdom are lost to future generations because we do not routinely compile a personal legacy document. What a shame! It's time for a new paradigm. Personal legacy writing should be part of everyone's later years.

It turns out you don't have to be an experienced writer to create a rich trove of short pieces that reflect your thoughts and feelings about what life has meant to you.

1

In the Elderwriters approach, we explore a wide range of forms—anecdotes, epiphanies, paragraphs and poems, lessons learned, one-liners, lists, letters, essays, and more—to help you collect your thoughts and celebrate your life.

WHAT IS A PERSONAL LEGACY DOCUMENT (PLD)?

> A **personal legacy document** is a collection of original and/or otherwise authored writings that reflect your thoughts and feeling about what life has meant to you. It is a gift to give to friends, family, and future generations.

I think of a PLD as a scrapbook of writings—a mosaic, a collage, a tapestry. It is a combination of family history, fond memories, and personal wisdom. The content is impressionistic: thoughts, feelings, positions taken, opinions held. What defining moments have brought you to where you are today? How have you made sense of your life? You're not just looking back, you're looking in.

If you think of your life as a smorgasbord, you could write about every dish in great detail or you could pick a few morsels to write about. We're morsel pickers.

The PLD is a new concept in legacy writing. You need an example. **Before you go any further, turn to Appendix E and peruse the *Sample Personal Legacy Document*.** It will give you a feel for the potential of this new form.

WHAT A PERSONAL LEGACY DOCUMENT IS **NOT**

A PLD is not a legal document. It does not replace your legal will. It is not a traditional memoir or autobiography. It is not something to mass produce or sell.

WHY CREATE A PERSONAL LEGACY DOCUMENT?

Good question. I have several good answers.

- » Writer, know thyself. Personal legacy writing forces you to be introspective, to consolidate and clarify your thoughts. What matters? What is your philosophy? It's a good exercise.

- » Personal legacy writing is a creative intellectual activity—good for the brain. You're not a spectator; you're a player.

- » Because the Elderwriters approach encourages you to work with others, writing, which can be an isolating activity, becomes a social one.

- » You will preserve some family history.

» You will have a gift to leave to future generations.

» A PLD is good fodder for a eulogy.

» The timing is right. Many of you are retired and have time to work on a personal legacy document.

» The technology is available. The computer and your local copy shop make the mechanics of creating and duplicating your document easy and inexpensive.

» Personal legacy writing may become a launch for other endeavors—other writing classes or facilitating an Elderwriters class yourself.

» Last, and possibly most important, your PLD will be a primary source of information about you—the real deal—about you, by you.

Key Feature of the Elderwriters Approach to Personal Legacy Writing—Short Pieces

Most of you are not professional, or even amateur, writers. You are folks who have something to say about life in general and your own lives in particular. There are things you would like to say to loved ones, past, present, and future; important events you would like to document; wisdom you would like to share.

How do you do that if you are not an experienced writer? Traditional memoir and autobiographical writing demand time, skill, and a patient reader. Fortunately you are not limited to those traditional forms. Try something new—be proactive, be adventurous, be creative. As Apple Computer has urged us, "Think Different".

At the heart of the Elderwriters approach to personal legacy writing are **short pieces**—sometimes as short as a couple of lines, rarely longer than a page or two.

There are several advantages to short pieces.

» Short pieces are manageable. The planning, organizing, and writing are not overwhelming. They focus on one concept. You get in and get out fast.

» Short pieces are easy to read. You won't bore your audience with long-winded renderings.

» Short pieces are in step with today's face-paced electronic world.

» Short pieces allow you to vary the landscape of your document. You will create a visually appealing array of pieces with artful use of fonts, shapes, and white space.

Short pieces are a can-do kind of writing.

I am an advocate for short pieces: a style of legacy writing that has been more or less absent from American culture but could draw many more people into legacy writing. Most inexperienced writers don't want to tackle a ten-page story—but some do. If you are new to legacy writing and find that longer pieces suit you, go for it. Use short pieces to complement your stories and create a PLD of your work. Short pieces aren't a requirement, they're a good idea. Whatever works for you, works.

VARYING THE FORMAT OF YOUR WRITINGS

In the Elderwriters approach, you are encouraged to break away from traditional prose. The "creative" in Creative Personal Legacy Writing includes selecting a format for each piece that enhances its meaning, tone, and presentation. Varying the written landscape adds depth and richness to your work, gives more options for self-expression, showcases your sense of humor, and draws the attention of the reader.

Below is a list of the nearly twenty-five writing formats we cover. Add your own. Different formats serve different topics for different people at different times.

- » Chapter 2—Sayings, songs, quotations, and prayers
- » Chapter 3—Paragraphs, vignettes, and narratives
- » Chapter 4—Embellished lists
- » Chapter 5—Very short memoir pieces
- » Chapter 6—Poems
- » Chapter 7—Letters
- » Chapter 9—Family history pieces, personal legacy essays
- » Chapter 10—Short personal essays/personal statements
- » Chapter 11—Interviews/Q and A, anecdotes, dialogues, one-liners, micro-memoirs
- » Chapter 12—Ethical wills, apologies, regrets, eulogies, obituaries

Keep in mind that your PLD is not limited to pieces you have written yourself. The list of formats may remind you of letters, poems, songs, or prayers authored by others that you would like to include to complement your own pieces.

AN OVERVIEW OF PLD CONTENT

This book is filled with exercises, suggestions, and examples of ideas for the content of your PLD. The content falls into six broad categories. To avoid feeling overwhelmed right off the bat, take your highlighter and highlight those topics that catch your eye, that seem to apply to you, that speak to your life. You want to find your comfort zone. Your highlights will provide valuable starting points for your pieces.

1. **Fond Memories:** Family holidays, childhood memories, rites of passage, military experiences, encounters with nature, sports triumphs, religious awakenings, professional accolades, performance events

2. **Family History:** Traditions, family trees, heritage, immigration/ethnicity, family business, heirlooms, biographies, anecdotes

3. **Personal Wisdom:** Values and beliefs, preferences and priorities, views and opinions, responses to setbacks and obstacles, apologies and regrets, hopes and aspirations

4. **Selections by Others:** Poems, sayings, songs, prayers, quotations, letters, the occasional cartoon

5. **Copies of Family Documents, Letters, and Commendations:** Immigration papers, legal certificates, awards, telegrams, personal letters, newspaper articles

6. **Combinations of 1—5:** Some of your finest and most memorable work will be pieces that encompass more than one category. Let your creativity shine!

Here's an additional list of Basic Themes and Special Topics. Put a Post-it on this page and return to it as you work through the exercises in later chapters.

BASIC THEMES AND SPECIAL TOPICS

Basic Themes

Aging	Lessons Learned
Apologies	Life
Grief/Loss	Love
Guidelines for Living	Marriage/Relationships
Family	Professional Life
Friendships	Recreation/Leisure
Health	Religion/Spirituality
Joy/Humor	Values and Beliefs

Special Topics

Awards	Music/Art
Cooking/Gardening	Pets
Education	Photography
Environment	Politics
Gay Rights	Reading/Writing
Government	Sports
Heroes	Technology
Hobbies	Theater/Acting

Holidays	TV
Illness	Vacations
Military	Volunteer/Community Service
Money	Yoga/Meditation

There's plenty of room here to add your own topics as you think of them.

📖 ☑ CHECKLIST OF PIECES

The following checklist should be helpful as you begin your legacy writing. Nothing is carved in stone, but it always helps to have a roadmap.

- ☐ Title Page
- ☐ Opening Letter
- ☐ Epigram/Epigraph
- ☐ List of Favorites
- ☐ Soothe Your Senses Poem
- ☐ Sayings, Quotations, Songs, Prayers by Others
- ☐ Pieces about Loved Ones Who Have Passed On
- ☐ Pieces about Loved Ones Still Here
- ☐ Pieces about Family History, Heirlooms, Treasures, Recipes
- ☐ Pieces about Your Family and Its Role in the Person You Are Today
- ☐ Pieces about What Matters to You, What's Important, What Gets You Fired Up
- ☐ Your Thoughts on Philosophical Themes—Love, Marriage, Friendship, Death, Religion, Justice
- ☐ The Impact of Historical Events on Your Life
- ☐ Personal Trials and Tribulations, Overcoming Adversity
- ☐ Some Fun Pieces Strategically Placed Throughout Your Document
- ☐ Any Photos or Family Documents You Wish to Include
- ☐ Closing Letter

▰ Helpful Hints for the Elderwriter

Here are some suggestions that may make your writing experience a little easier.

» Find a place to write—a favorite chair, a quiet corner where you can work undisturbed.

» Keep a dictionary and thesaurus nearby. (There are many websites that can help you find synonyms, antonyms, and rhyming words. If you are online, try wordhippo.com.)

» It doesn't take long to forget a good idea. Write it down. Keep a pen and notepad in your pocket or purse, in the car, and at strategic locations around the house—the nightstand next to your bed is critical.

» I don't particularly mind the decline in cigar smoking, but it means cigar boxes are in short supply. Where does one keep one's treasures these days? You need a place to store bits of writing, newspaper clippings, and photos you think will come in handy. Try a hinged shoebox.

» Be brief. "Vigorous writing is concise." (Strunk and White, 2000) You don't want to ramble. Figure out what you want to say and say it. Try to eliminate sentences that don't support your main point. It is said that in a letter to a friend, Blaise Pascal apologized, saying, "I have made this letter longer than usual because I lack the time to make it shorter." Take the time. Everyone appreciates a well-crafted short piece.

» You may be able to compose right on the computer. I can't. But I do try to type up my handwritten pieces at regular intervals. It's easier to edit and revise a piece if it looks nice.

» If you don't own a computer with a word processing program, you may want to see if the public library, friends, or family members can help you out. A computer isn't required, but it will make your life a little easier. Then again, hand-written pieces have a special intimacy. Some people prefer them.

» I am a firm believer that Elderwriters can create a handsome, engaging, informative personal legacy document without any additional reading or training. This is a come-as-you-are endeavor. For some people, however, the research and reconnaissance work are part of the fun. In response to their needs, I have organized a list of books I used to prepare the Elderwriters course. For those of you who would like a reading list, it is in Appendix B.

» Take your time. Look at photo albums. Ask friends and family if they have any suggestions. Locate those scraps of paper you've squirreled away over the years with bits of songs, poems, and quotations. Find pieces you've written in the past. Gather up any family documents you've been saving. Reread the Sample PLD in Appendix E.

CAUTIONS

1. You don't want to say anything hurtful. Celebrate your life! Your legacy document is not the place to air grievances or launch personal attacks. Put those somewhere else.

2. We all run up against memories that make us sad. Some of them are things we have chosen not to think about or resolve for many years. You don't have to go there if you don't want to. Omissions are acceptable. On the other hand, you may decide this is an opportunity for a healthy catharsis—that difficult times have helped shape your character. It is not uncommon for participants to cry when reading a heartfelt piece. It's all part of looking back and looking in.

3. If you are working in a group, you need to be concerned about **confidentiality.** Legacy writing often leads to personal disclosures. What happens in the group stays in the group. You want to protect yourself and your colleagues. That being said, it is everyone's responsibility to draw the line between personal and private. Don't overburden the group with information that is none of their business. You may have some pieces that are appropriate for your document but not for the group.

✍ START-UP EXERCISES

You want to build up a little momentum right away. Writing generates more writing. These start-up exercises often give rise to ideas for additional pieces. Refer back to them as you work your way through the guide.

✍ EXERCISE I. A FEW OF YOUR FAVORITE THINGS

Let's try something. Here's a good place to start: the grossly underrated **list**—probably the most accessible literary form there is. Make a list of 20—25 of your favorite things, just one or two words each. It's as simple as that.

I love these lists. They say so much about you with a minimum of time and effort. There are always a few surprises in them. They make a great piece to put in your PLD.

✑ Exercise 2. The Senses

Now that you've made a list of your favorite things, write a poem or set of sentences that catalogs those things that soothe your senses, your soul. These are important elements of your personality. Share them.

The sight of _____ .

The sound of _____ .

The feel of _____ .

The taste of _____ .

The thought of _____ .

Here is an example of a senses piece that was written by a woman who claimed she had never done any creative writing.

Things That Soothe My Senses

The sight of spring flowers, the sky at sunset, and my children soothe my senses.

The sound of the ocean waves, mummy playing the piano, and the loons on Pollywog Pond soothe my senses.

The feel of the sun on my face, Cloud's soft fur, and my husband Sandy's hand in mine soothe my senses.

The taste of English Cucumber, Sponge Candy, and hot black sweetened tea with milk soothe my senses.

The smell of my lavender garden, newly mown grass, and breakfast cooking on the campfire soothe my senses.

The thought of my children happy and healthy, spending time with them, and traveling the journey of life with my love, Sandy soothe my senses.

Chapter 2

Getting Started

In Chapter 2 you will:

- » assemble sayings, songs, quotations, and prayers that have had special meaning for you over the years
- » identify family documents you would like to include with your writings
- » experiment with two exercises to help you access your memories and organize your thoughts

---

CHAPTER 2 CONTINUES YOUR INTRODUCTION to personal legacy writing. It is easier to gather up the words of others than to write your own. We start there. This is also a good time to locate any family documents you would like to include in your PLD.

Then we move on to two exercises to help you access your memories and organize your thoughts. You will use them over and over as you create your PLD.

Sayings, Songs, Quotations, and Prayers

Not all the words in your PLD have to be your own. We all have a few sayings, songs, quotations, or prayers that have stuck with us over the years. These stock phrases are part of the infrastructure of our everyday lives. Some of them have been handed down from parents and grandparents, some are clipped from newspapers, some are lines from books and movies. We use them again and again to simplify our world, share insights, express emotions, and justify actions.

✍ EXERCISE 3. YOUR COLLECTION OF SAYINGS

Put together a little collection of your favorite **sayings** that you can draw on as your legacy writing moves forward. These one-liners will provide inspiration, clarification, and enhancement to your work.

Examples:

» Albert Finney on being asked how he felt about turning 70: "I don't think about my age. I think about my time—and my time is now."

» Life's messy.

» The only behavior you really can change is your own.

» Be brave.

Add favorite songs or prayers to your collection. You'll find a place for them down the line.

📖 DOCUMENTS WITHIN YOUR DOCUMENT

Today's technology makes this a great time to create a personal legacy document. Cherished memorabilia—marriage licenses, certificates of all kinds, letters and telegrams, immigration papers, newspaper clippings—can be scanned by your home printer or local copy shop. You will have inexpensive, good-quality replicas without damaging the originals. Although your PLD is primarily a record of your own thoughts and words, the inclusion of carefully selected family documents can complement your work.

To my knowledge, other than photos, my family did not retain any of the aforementioned memorabilia. Maybe there wasn't anything to save. Families vary. My PLD is a first!

🚐 HELPFUL HINTS: TWO EXERCISES FOR ACCESSING YOUR MEMORIES AND ORGANIZING YOUR THOUGHTS

1. A Memory Retrieval Exercise

Most of what you want to say in your PLD is already in your mind. We are not so much creators as re-creators.

Some of the pieces you write for your document will be verbal descriptions of special memories—family holidays, rites of passage, military experiences, encounters with nature, sports triumphs, religious awakenings, final hours with a loved one—moments you would like to recapture for your document. How do you get images from the background of your memory into the foreground so you can write about them?

Here is a short retrieval exercise to help you mentally re-create memories you want to write about. The more completely you can picture the event, the easier the writing will be. We write what we see. Also concentrate on the sensory and emotional details of the memory.

To maximize the effectiveness of the exercise, I suggest the following:

» Read through the meditation several times before you start, so you are familiar with the procedure.

» Find a quiet spot where you can sit comfortably.

» Pick a time when you feel relaxed and unhurried.

» Turn off your cell phone.

» Have a pencil and paper nearby.

A MEMORY RETRIEVAL EXERCISE

Slowly relax into your chair: accept its support.
Let go of any tension in your body.
Lean back and close your eyes.
Breathe deeply—In…out. In…out.

Think about the memory you wish to reclaim. Imagine that you are quietly watching it unfold in front of you. Take your time.

As more of the scene becomes visible, you pick up sounds; you see colors and shadows.

Where are you? What's going on? Who's there? Watch and listen.

Now slowly put yourself into the scene.
Turn completely around. Scan the outer edges.
Move to the center. Mingle. Note the faces, the colors, the textures, the smells, the sounds.
What is the tone of the event? How do you feel?
Examine your emotions.

Allow yourself to be part of the reenactment of this memory. Relive the experience. Feel the feelings.

When you are ready, open your eyes and begin to write.

I didn't know my maternal grandparents very well. We only saw them once a year, in the summer. Their lifestyle was quite different from my family's. With the help of the retrieval exercise, I was able to recall many details I hadn't thought about in years.

> *They ate breakfast in the dining room...the smell of bacon and molasses cookies...Grandma had a hot tray to keep things warm...all this for a toast-and-peanut-butter kid; I was dazzled...my grandfather went by his initials, L.K.... he wore a tie every day of his life...Grandma had a scar on her thumb...Barb and I slept on an ancient sofa bed—horribly uncomfortable...the bedroom had a night light with a tiny purple iris inside the bulb...Grandma sang Methodist hymns in a deep, rich alto voice; L.K. accompanied her on the piano—just the black keys; I was fascinated by their camaraderie...it was very quiet there, unlike our home on Route 20—like being on another planet...to this day, when I smell hand cream with lanolin, I think of Madge W. Brown.*

✎ EXERCISE 4. USING THE MEMORY RETRIEVAL EXERCISE

Use the memory retrieval exercise to help you resurrect the details of a special event in your life you would like to write about. At this point, just worry about gathering the data. Later, your written account may take any form—a paragraph, vignette, narrative, poem, letter; you'll find your comfort zone.

2. Clustering/Mind-Mapping

One of the Elderwriters suggested using clustering as a way of freeing up our thoughts and combating writer's block. It has become a popular and useful tool.

Clustering—aka **mind-mapping**—is a stress free strategy to help you focus, recall, and organize your thoughts. This brainstorming technique encourages you to free associate ideas. It puts your inner landscape right out in front of you.

Here's the process:

» Start with a topic of interest. Place that word or phrase in the center of a blank sheet of paper.

» Next comes the brainstorming phase. Take five to ten minutes and jot down whatever comes into your mind about the topic, creating branches around the center word that give rise to even more associations.

» Lastly, try to identify patterns or themes in your maze of information. There may not be any. That's okay, too.

Good to know:

» You don't have to use everything in the cluster, and/or you can add more ideas later.

» Clustering can lead to any literary form—poetry, paragraphs, essays, letters, etc. It's a good all-purpose brainstorming activity.

In class, we tried clustering around the word **America**.

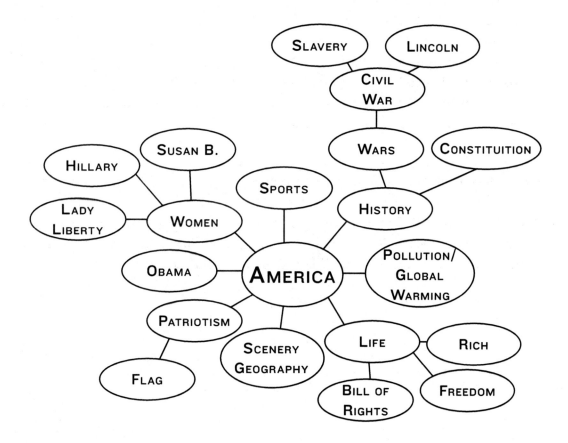

The exercise helped generate the poem below.

MY AMERICA

The beautiful
Give me your tired, your poor…
The land of unlimited possibilities
Admired, imitated, copied, envied
A place in the Sun—Elizabeth Taylor, Montgomery Clift
The greatest Show on Earth—Cornell Wilde
The land of the free
Except for the slaves
The Deep South
Charleston—noblesse oblige
Land masses, oil, gold, railroads
Move over, away, Chief Joseph
In God we trust
Most helpful people on earth
Most impressive sights—The Grand Tetons, Yellowstone Park,
    Niagara Falls, New York, Chicago, San Francisco, New Orleans
Who would want to be anyplace else?

✍ EXERCISE 5. A CLUSTERING ACTIVITY

Try doing the clustering/mind-mapping exercise on a topic of your choice—a friend, sibling, other relative, holiday tradition, a concept from the basic themes list—then organize your data to create a piece. Put your own personal spin on it.

CHAPTER 3

COMFORTABLE WRITING

IN CHAPTER 3 YOU WILL:

» consider using paragraphs, vignettes, and narratives in your writing

» reflect on Martin Gardner's *ah, aha,* and *haha* moments

» review short profiles of some of our Elderwriters

THIS GUIDE DOES NOT ATTEMPT to teach you to write. Elderwriters is a come-as-you-are approach. Whatever basic writing skills you bring to the table will work just fine. What I *can* help you with is becoming a better, more creative personal legacy writer. Selecting a format for your pieces is an unfamiliar task. I want to make sure you are aware of your options. In Chapter 3 we look at paragraphs, vignettes, and narratives along with samples of participant work.

PARAGRAPHS, VIGNETTES, AND NARRATIVES

Paragraph: The **paragraph** is the fundamental unit of composition. A paragraph consists of several sentences that are grouped together to discuss one subject.

Wesley Kobylak's work is always a treat. This deceptively simple paragraph about fishing is part of a larger piece titled, *Things I Have Learned.*

"Fishing should be quiet, like meditation. It's the water, the fish, and you. You have to know the difference between a nibble and a bite. You can't set the hook on a nibble. You have to learn not to get excited. It's all patience, you put the fish out of your mind."

VIGNETTE

A **vignette** is a short descriptive or impressionistic literary sketch that focuses on one moment or gives particular insight into a character, idea, or setting.

Tuesday Morning is a vignette by Diane Drysdale. She could see this scene in her mind's eye as clearly as if she were standing there today. Her artful description reads like a pastel.

TUESDAY MORNING

The morning sun glistened through the dining room windowpanes. Petey squawked and fluttered, making his presence known, but rarely sharing his thoughts with us. It was Tuesday morning and so the ironing board was set up and Grama was seated behind it, rhythmically going about the work of smoothing wrinkles from Monday's clean clothes. She had a steady and persistent hand that succeeded in a finished piece to be worn with pride. Even underpants were smoothed and folded to stack neatly in a bureau drawer. Blouses hung on wire hangers blossomed along the side of the ironing board. Grama was sitting, not singing along but quietly turning out a quality product. It was taken as a matter of course. Worn clothes dropped down the laundry chute would soon reappear ready and crisp for another week of school and play.

Vignettes have been a popular vehicle for describing friends and relatives. Here is a tribute to Elderwriter Helgi Mepham's father.

MENS SANA IN CORPORE SANO

Translated from Latin to English it means: a sound mind in a sound body. Throughout my growing-up years my father spoke to me of the meaning of this saying and guided me by example.

He had been a talented athlete and was active all through his life, living until the age of 93 and ½.

Depending on what country occupied Estonia, the main language in school would be changed. My dad was fluent in Russian, German, and Estonian. Upon arriving in America at the age of 49, English was a new challenge for him. It did not take him long to master this language also. He would listen to the radio, read lots of books, and pick ten new words most days, learn the meaning of these words, and use them in sentences. He also loved to write. I still have so many letters in his own handwriting. Every so often, I sit down in a comfy chair and read some of them. They bring back so many good memories.

My dad also kept up on current events and took great pleasure in quizzing us when we visited. He was an amazing man and a wonderful father.

Elderwriter Gwen K. Tucker wrote this vignette about her great-grandfather.

POPPY

The minister—Rev. S. H. McKay
From the pulpit, a huge presence with a booming voice.
A six-year-old could imagine it the voice of God on Sunday morning.

The patriarch—Papa
A wagon trip from Missouri launched the McKay family in Russell, KS.
Four of his five children and all of the next two generations were born there. He made predictions for babies' futures, and bought burial plots for wives, children, and grand-children.
A respectful community attended his funeral.

The great-grandfather—Poppy.
Sometimes called Papoo-pie-GMC, he loved pie and his fast careening truck.
He could be forceful with others, with an angry "Thunderation!"
But gentle with great-grands; we could find lemon drops in the chest pocket of his over-alls.
Evenings, he rocked his chair beside the coal-burning stove and smoked his pipe.

The provider—Papa, Poppy, Papoo-pie-GMC; so many talents.
From the peach trees beside the house, he sold (or gave) to everyone; we ate on the spot.
He butchered pigs from a pen north of town to feed us.
Any traveling Black folks could find sleeping space in his house.
He carved limestone for city parks; it's still there.
And preacher—pastor, minister, too, but preacher suits his style.

Memories of Sam McKay.

Few, but strong from the seven years in his house.

A huge presence and legacy in the family.

For this person, he helped set characteristics to find in a man: strong, generous, religious, worker/provider—and loving.

Note: "Thunderation" was his word when angry or frustrated. As a religious man, he wouldn't swear or cuss.

✎ EXERCISE 6. WRITING ABOUT SOMEONE YOU LOVE AND ADMIRE

One of the primary goals of personal legacy writing is to share with friends, family, and future generations what life has meant to you—who you are, what's important, what matters. What you say about the people you love and admire says a lot about you. Short vignettes can open a window onto your life while paying tribute to loved ones.

Reread Helgi Mepham's piece about her father and Gwen Tucker's piece about her great-grandfather. Think of a friend, relative, mentor, famous person, or pet you would like to honor with a piece in your legacy document. Give it a go.

No doubt, some of you can compose, revise, and edit right on the computer. If you are writing things out longhand—as I do—try this:

Partition a blank sheet of paper into six to eight strips.

① _____

② _____

③ _____

In each strip, write one or two sentences describing the individual, how you feel about him/her, and in what way that person made a difference in your life. (Use clustering if you have trouble getting started.) Don't worry about the order of the sentences—just write them down as they come into your mind.

Now cut the strips apart and rearrange them until you have one or two paragraphs you like. Type them up and you're good to go.

NARRATIVES

A **narrative** is a story or account of events or experiences. Narratives are not just descriptions. They go somewhere; they have forward motion; they tell a story. Narratives can be short or long. Here is a short one.

1996

One Friday night in late October, I met Gram and Grandad at Ripa's to celebrate my birthday. The conversation meandered around until Gram announced, "I've joined TAP." Somewhat incredulous, I asked, "You're dancing?"

Her face lit up and she laughed like a schoolgirl. "No, no," she sputtered. "It's the Telephone Assistance Program."

I realized I hadn't seen her laugh like that in a very long time.

I never saw her again. She died in her sleep on Thanksgiving night. We had planned to meet for brunch at Bob Evan's in Batavia on Friday. She stood me up.

This longer narrative is by Helen Crews. Helen has written several pieces about her early years in New York City.

THE UNBIRTHDAY PARTY

The argument in the boxy steel elevator was getting out of hand and I was losing. School had let out and I was returning to our apartment on the seventh floor of the projects when I became embroiled in a heated dispute over some silly childish argument about which I can't even remember. You've got to realize the subject of dispute was unimportant to a kid. What was important was that you prove to hold your own either verbally or physically in any given situation. God help the poor slob who couldn't; he/she became the brunt of any smartaleck's heartless remarks that were dished out like servings of codliver oil you were forced to swallow. I was alone, so I had no sisters or friends to give needed moral support as we exchanged zingers and this cocky Spanish kid I didn't recognize as living in the projects and his two sisters were really getting the best of me. I had to say or do something decisive to end the sparring in my favor.

So I confidently told them that they couldn't attend my birthday party that evening because they had been unfriendly and rude to me. You should have seen the look of despair and shock that collectively came over their faces. Miss a party? Their behavior changed abruptly, but it was too late. My floor had arrived and I marched triumphantly off the elevator and strode proudly to my apartment. The rest of the evening was uneventful until the doorbell rang. I opened the door widely with my mother standing inquisitively behind me, to see to my complete surprise and dismay the kids I had argued with earlier, dressed in their Sunday best with gifts in their arms! I don't know who felt worse, me or the kids who stood there sparkling like manikins in a Macy's show window at Easter. With much chagrin, I admitted that I had lied; there was no party and no birthday.

There are eight million stories in the naked city. This has been one of them.

I'm sure you're beginning to get a sense of the variety and richness of these short legacy pieces. This is just the tip of the iceberg.

📁 THE *AH*, THE *AHA*, AND THE *HAHA* MOMENT

Perhaps you remember the popular mathematics and science writer, Martin Gardner (1914-2010). He wrote the Mathematical Games column in *Scientific American* for twenty-five years. Gardner talked about the *ah,* the *aha,* and the *haha* moment. He was speaking mathematically—which most of us are not—but it's a good way to think about the moments we want to capture in our legacy writing.

» ah—the satisfying and peaceful moments; moments of accomplishment

» aha!—moments of insight and discovery

» haha—the funny stuff

You all have them—the stories you tell over and over. The little treasures you've been keeping in your heart. Write them down. Let them speak for you. Let them remind your reader what your life was all about. That's personal legacy writing!

Here's one of my favorite *haha* moments.

Marianne and I were neighbors on the 3rd floor of Wilson Magnet High School for more than 15 years. One afternoon I covered a class for Marianne. I was wearing a favorite outfit—black-watch plaid pleated skirt, navy blue sweater, and white turtleneck—probably thought I looked pretty sharp. As I was expounding on the consequences of the Industrial Revolution, a young girl in the front row piped up:

"That's a Catholic skirt, isn't it?"

✍ EXERCISE 7. KEEPING A LIST OF AH, AHA, AND HAHA MOMENTS

The *ah, aha, and haha* are everyday moments that stand out in your mind—the extraordinary in the ordinary. For now, just keep a running list of these moments. Wait to write them up until you have a few more formats under your belt.

⚏ Helpful Hints: Split Them Up

If a piece seems to be getting long and unmanageable, it may be that you're dealing with material for two pieces—related, but distinct with respect to time, perspective, or tone. Place them under a common title and separate the two pieces with a snazzy little ๛. (See Wingdings in Chapter 8.)

📖 Elderwriter Profiles

This section on Document Construction contains short profiles of a few Elderwriters participants. I thought you might like to know a little bit about them, what formats they used, and why they were creating a PLD. Most of them made multiple copies of their document at a local copy shop to share with friends and family.

Elderwriter Profiles

1. Ed: 87—a retired university engineer. He wrote one-to-two page narratives, a short play, a poem. Ed was writing his document for his grandchildren. He wanted to share a way of life they didn't even know existed eighty years ago.

2. Helen: 69—a retired math teacher. Helen included one page narratives, lists, quotes, personal essays, poems, songs, family documents, letters, anecdotes. Her PLD was for her children.

3. Kathleen: 67—a retired music teacher. She included one-to-two page narratives, a prose poem, other poems, newspaper articles, family letters and documents in her PLD. She was writing for her children and herself.

4. Liz:— a retired urban school public relations specialist. She was writing to share her life with her step-children. Liz used short narratives, personal essays, and letters.

5. Liz:—a nurse. Liz showed very creative use of formats—poems, spreadsheet, lists, personal essays, six word memoirs. She was writing for herself.

6. Fritz:—Liz's husband. Fritz tried poems, lists, narratives. Totally new to writing, he was a real trooper.

7. Marcia:—a retired dancer and world traveler. Marcia wrote mostly two-to-three page narratives. She was writing for her daughters.

8. Sharon:—a housewife/caretaker, mom. Sharon wrote poems, lists, personal essays, letters. She was creating a PLD for her husband who was losing his memory because of surgery.

9. Karolina: 70—a retired language teacher. Karolina used lists, family documents, letters, poems, narratives, anecdotes. She created the document for her children.

10. Barb: in her 80's. She created a document of vignettes titled "Women in My Life".

11. Mary:—a housewife. Mary created an elegant scrapbook/PLD—personal essays, lists, letters, quotes, pieces by other authors.

12. Barb: 78—retired housewife/fundraiser for non-profits. Barb used dialogs, poems, anecdotes, quotes, personal narratives, letters. The PLD was for her daughters.

13. Wesley: 63—an accomplished writer and college professor. Wesley wrote poems, interviews, lists, personal essays. He is working on a document for his children.

✍ EXERCISE 8. WILD CARD ☺

The Wild Card allows you to ignore the constraints of my suggestions and create your own exercise. Go for it!

CHAPTER 4

PRACTICAL WRITING

IN CHAPTER 4 YOU WILL:

» encounter a frequently used format—the embellished list

» begin working on a Guidelines for Living piece

» start to prepare a table of contents for your PLD

» pick up a few helpful hints

How's it going? Here are some typical reactions at this point.

» You're loving every minute of this.

» Your mind is racing so fast you can't get your ideas sorted out.

» You completed exercises 1 and 2, made lots of notes, and are now waiting for an inspiration.

» You found some writing you did twenty years ago and are stuck there.

» You want to create a PLD, but it's hard. This feels like work that isn't going very well.

Don't give up! You'll find your stride. I have a treat for you—the embellished list.

◧ THE EMBELLISHED LIST

The **embellished list** is the duct tape of personal legacy writing—multipurpose, dependable, flexible. It frequently saves the day. Rare is the PLD that doesn't contain at least one embellished list.

You encountered the simple list in Exercise 1—one- or two-word entries, no embellishment. Some situations require more explanation—not paragraphs, but a couple of sentences of definition, detail, or commentary. Listing allows you to avoid transition sentences. You don't have to worry about gliding seamlessly from one paragraph to the next. You just list.

Let me give you some examples.

Elderwriters often want to write about their travel experiences. The embellished list allows you to document highlights without becoming boring. The following travel list contained nine entries. Here are three of them.

EUROPEAN TRAVELS

June—September 1959—American Field Service foreign exchange student to Zeven, Germany. I sailed on the Holland American "Groote Bear" across the Atlantic Ocean to LaHavre, France, then through the English Channel to Rotterdam, Holland. I traveled by train to Dusseldorf, Germany, and then to Bremen, where I was met by my family.

April 1995—Katie and I went with the Rochester Philharmonic Youth Orchestra on a tour to England where we stayed with a family in Worthing. There were rehearsals and concerts in various venues, including a concert in Arundel Cathedral and St. James' s Church in London. We also visited Brighton Beach.

July 2001—Third Presbyterian Chancel Choir was the "choir in residence" for a week in Rochester, England. We sang Evensong every day at 4:00 PM. We also traveled to Canterbury Cathedral. The second week we sang various concerts and traveled to Bath, Stratford-on-Avon, Salisbury, Coventry, and Oxford, ending with a day in London.

Pets are a favorite subject. They may have played an important role in difficult times. They are a source of joy, comfort, and shared memories.

OUR PETS

Trixie—adorable, peppy, mixed breed with mixed instincts, loving, needy

Kitty—independent, patient, tolerant, good genes, resilient

Tucker—handsome tabby with green eyes, often confused, affectionate, a good friend, named after Tuckernuck Island

Bubbles—definite, stubborn, a good hunter, territorial, adaptable when forced to be, sensitive

Sunshine—Pretty yellow bird, good singer, short-lived in a fancy home

Mr. B—club mascot, suffered through a lonely winter after Kari's death, rescued by Shelly and spent the rest of his life in pet heaven with the kids at Park School.

Here are two excerpts from Liz Rowsick's embellished list.

FAMILY, FRIENDS AND OTHER IMPORTANT PEOPLE
QUOTES TURNED INTO LIFE TRANSACTIONS

The father of three of my sons one day inadvertently said something that caught my attention and I repeat it to myself on days when things are difficult or not as good as they should be or when something can go either way. We had moved into a new home in a new town and we were noticing how dark the sky was in one direction and how bright the sun was shining in another and he said:
"IT ALL DEPENDS ON WHICH WINDOW YOU LOOK OUT."

A professor of mine from Roberts Wesleyan said this during class one evening and his words have made me stop and think many, many times. He said:
"THERE ARE ALWAYS OPTIONS. STATUS QUO IS AN OPTION."

One participant used the embellished list in a light-hearted piece about the evolution of the telephone over her lifetime, from the party line to the iPhone. It was a bit of history most of us had forgotten.

GUIDELINES FOR LIVING—A VARIATION ON THE EMBELLISHED LIST

According to a 2011 Associated Press poll, a majority of the 77 million emerging baby boomers cite "the wisdom accumulated during their lives as the best thing about aging." This is your chance to share that wisdom. Every PLD should include a **Guidelines for Living** piece.

Your core values, challenged beliefs, and lessons learned explain the paths you have taken, the decisions you've made, the person you have become.

Elderwriter Bonnie Turchetti graciously agreed to share her Guidelines with us.

GUIDELINES FOR LIVING

These guidelines have been written to express my thoughts about the attitudes I consider to be important. In no way do I declare that I have followed them throughout my life. In fact, it has taken all my life to come to know and understand their importance. Once accepted and embraced, I strive each day to live by them.

Know Yourself

Think about *who* you are and want to be. Assess weaknesses, firm up assets, and aspire to develop qualities you admire.

Be Aware of Social and Political Issues

Good personhood and citizenship depend on awareness of issues. Be informed.

Base Decisions and Judgments on Evidence

Respect and Give Attention to Everyone's Opinion

Wisdom is often gained in unexpected ways from unexpected people.

Continue to Learn Throughout Life Until Your Last Conscious Breath

We just don't know what we don't know. Be open; the possibilities are endless.

Organize All Aspects of Your Life, It Frees You to Create

Be a Positive Force in the World. Speak Up for Worthy Causes

Be Brave

Self-knowledge can be a source of strength. Use it to overcome and accept life's challenges.

Let your voice be heard when slurs or disparaging remarks are made in your presence.

Have the courage of your convictions.

<u>Share Laughter</u>

<u>Be Kind</u>

and finally

<u>Share Love</u>

So many ways to do it
With children as they grow
With parents when we're younger
With friends we come to know
With smiles at strangers passing by
To let them know we care
About the world we live in
And that we see them there
So many ways to share our love with people everywhere
A nod, a wave, a gentle touch
A handshake when we meet
Sends messages to people
That often we repeat
They say "I see you, you're important"
We're all a part, you see
Of this grand world we live in
And love in, thoughtfully.

⟿⟾

My own guidelines are not as eloquent.

GUIDELINES AND INSIGHTS

Every now and then, I hear a statement, or have an insight, that I find myself returning to again and again. These guidelines have become an integral part of my personal decision making apparatus.

1. The only behavior you can change is your own.
2. If you don't want to do something, one reason is as good as another.
3. If you don't like your life, change it.
4. Find something that will bring joy to your life.
5. You can accomplish as much as you want as long as you don't care who gets the credit.

29

6. You can learn more by listening than by talking.
7. People do the best they can under the circumstances.
8. A sense of entitlement is the root of much evil.
9. Mediocrity is not a behavioral constraint.
10. The John Henry Conjecture: Don't fight technology—technology will win.
11. Expect variation.
12. Look backward 20% and forward 80%.

Here is a list by Doris M. Meadows

Words I Live By

1. Always we begin again.
2. It is never too late.
3. Love is everything.
4. Faith is hope in the unseen.
5. The opposite of love is not hate but fear.
6. As long as we are alive, we are becoming ourselves.

Some participants in my classes have expressed their guidelines in paragraph form as a personal creed or manifesto. Others have incorporated them into an opening letter.

✍   ## Exercise 9. Set up a Guidelines for Living file.

This page will be a work-in-progress for some time. Revisit your collection of sayings and quotations. Write down the one-liners you use over and over. Consider the beliefs you hold that motivate your actions and influence the way you treat others. Return to this page regularly until you are satisfied that it accurately represents your personal outlook. Then type it up and put it in the completed pile.

📖   ## Setting Up a Table of Contents

You are preparing a document that will be read for decades, generations. It will outlast your legal will and most photo albums. It will be quoted at special occasions and family events. This is how you will be remembered. What do you want to say?

Whether or not you choose to include a table of contents in your document, it is a valuable—I would say, indispensable—organizational step along the way. Rarely does the table of contents emerge full blown, all at once. It will evolve over time as you gather your thoughts.

The clustering exercise can be helpful here. Cluster around "contents". See what you come up with. Don't forget pieces you may have written in the past—eulogies, special journal entries, letters, or poems.

In writing, as in speaking, some of us use more words than others. Rose Booth had a few things to say, and she said them.

TABLE OF CONTENTS

1. Welcome letter
2. I remember world events
3. Views on aging and life in general
4. A word on religion
5. Leaving letter

This is the final version of one participant's table of contents.

CONTENTS

Cover Letter to David and Katie
Facts About Myself
Prayers, Quotes, Poetry
    Soothing the Soul/Senses
What Christmas Means to Me
Music as a Theme in My Life
Travel as a Theme in My Life
My Childhood
    Scenes From My Childhood
    High School Honors
Hobbies and Play
    Sewing
    Square Dancing
Volunteer Activities
    RAIHN, Laotian family
My Life Going Forward

I made a list of topics I wanted to cover and created a manila folder for each topic.

I have added other pieces, but this was my starting point.

Guidelines
A Few of my Favorite Things
On Marriage/Relationships
God, Religion, Spirituality
Death, Burial, and the Hereafter
Professional Life
The Military

Fellow Elderwriter, Doris M. Meadows, who has been writing most of her life, had this Table of Contents.

Preface: Happy Memories
I. Family Heritage
    A. The Great Aunts
    B. A Box of Cherries
    C. California Dream—A Picture
    D. For Alex—The Two Days of Your Birth
    E. For Clarice—The Day You Were Born
    F. For Lucia—The Night You Were Born
    G. Remembering Family—Brief Snapshots of Beloved Ancestors
II. My Life in Stories
    A. Where I Came From
    B. Growing Up With Cousins Downstairs
    C. Extended Family Extends
    D. A Captured Moment
    E. Snapshots of Work
    F. How I Met Your Father
    G. Winning the Lottery—A Poem
    H. A Wedding to Remember
    I. The PhD Adventure
    J. Op-Eds—My Crusades
III. My Writing
    A. Eulogy for Peter
    B. Eulogy for My Mother
    C. List of Published Writings
    D. Resignation Letter 2001
    E. Poetry
IV. My Last Resume
V. Words I Try to Live By and Favorite Wisdom

Listing the contents of your document will help you focus. Remember the smorgasbord. You're not going to write about everything that ever happened to you. Pick your morsels carefully. Make them count.

✍ EXERCISE 10. WRITING UP A PRELIMINARY TABLE OF CONTENTS

Write up a preliminary table of contents for your document. Consider involving other members of your family—children, spouse, siblings— in your legacy writing endeavor. Ask them what they would like to see included in your document.

🐢 HELPFUL HINTS: INPUT FROM FAMILY; YOUR AUDIENCE; PURPOSE AND TONE OF A PIECE

1. Family history is a popular topic. If you have created pieces about ancestors, consider using statements by other family members as an epigraph or sidebar. Canvass the grandchildren for one- or two-sentence thoughts/memoirs about the grandfather and grandmother. Not only will these opinions enhance your work, they will draw others into your project.

2. Creating a table of contents is one way to stay on task. Another way is to concentrate on your audience. For whom are you writing this document? Yourself? Your children? Family? Friends? What are your goals? A well-defined audience will help focus your efforts and guide your writing.

3. In the Elderwriters approach to personal legacy writing, we do not diagram sentences, correct punctuation, or rigorously analyze the characteristics of a written piece. It's simply not necessary. However, a little time spent thinking about the purpose of a piece and the tone you wish to set will help you choose words and create images that support your intentions. Attention to purpose and tone may also guide your choice of format.

Here are some common purposes for legacy pieces:

» to analyze or interpret

» to celebrate

» to commemorate

» to describe or inform

» to document

» to eulogize

» to honor or revere

- » to mourn
- » to question
- » to reflect
- » to reminisce

These words describe a tone or mood you might want to create with your piece:

- » amused
- » assertive
- » awed
- » concerned/angry
- » congratulatory
- » factual
- » inspired
- » nostalgic
- » pensive/thoughtful
- » reverent
- » sad
- » triumphant

Your PLD will be more robust and engaging if you vary the purpose and tone of your pieces to fit your own emotional landscape.

Put a Post-it on this section!

CHAPTER 5

FOCUS ON YOU

IN CHAPTER 5 YOU WILL:

» investigate the very short memoir piece format

» review content suggestions from earlier chapters

» pick up some hints

T HE MASTER OF THE VERY short memoir piece is Rochester's own Sonja Livingston. Ms. Livingston's award-winning book, *Ghostbread,* is a series of over one hundred short memoir pieces about growing up poor in Rochester, New York. It is a landmark in creative nonfiction. By all means, get yourself a copy.

THE VERY SHORT MEMOIR PIECE

An autobiography is the story of someone's life written by that person. The memoir is autobiographical but it is more affective, impressionistic, thoughtful. Memoirs usually target a particular period in a person's life. Joan Didion's *The Year of Magical Thinking,* about her life the year after her husband's death, is a memoir you may have read.

The **very short memoir piece** comes under the heading "brief creative nonfiction." I'm thinking of a piece 200—300 words in length. It could be even shorter. The piece is centered on one scene or episode from the past. It should have a personal touch, an intimacy. You are sharing a special memory with the reader.

A couple of very short memoir pieces will be a great addition to your PLD. Most of us don't have one hundred of these in us, but we all have one or two. Here are some samples from my classes.

MOM WAS A TWIN
BY EDWIN KINNEN

Mom was a twin, an identical twin—and that led to a lot of confusion. It even started back when they tricked Dad on a date with my Aunt Carrie when he thought he was with Mom. My sister and I never had a problem knowing which one was our Mom. If Dad ever did in the years after they were married, he never let on.

Aunt Carrie lived in a big city and we lived in a small nearby village. When she would visit us, this meant taking a streetcar, then a bus ride, and finally a short walk to our house. Back then, travel for a lady involved not Sunday best but good going-out clothes. When Aunt Carrie got to our house, she would change into one of Mom's well-worn cotton housedresses. Neighbors would see her out in our yard and speak to her not suspecting that she wasn't our Mom. Some afternoons, Aunt Carrie would lean over a sink on the far side of the kitchen wall to see if my sister and I could be fooled when we came in the door after school. We never were. Can't get around that Mom-kid bond.

2006: Minneapolis/St. Paul

The boys pick me up at the airport and drive to a diner for breakfast. Just the three of us, just the three of us. Hasn't happened in years.

They talk nonstop—almost oblivious to my presence—as if this reunion were the most natural thing in the world. They exude energy and intensity. The air vibrates around them. They are the most interesting people I know.

I am escorted into the restaurant—Zach with his signature watch cap, Vic rolling in at well over 200 pounds. I look like I'm being kidnapped. I feel safe.

They order enormous amounts of food. The waitress looks at me and smiles. I'm out of control. **"THESE ARE MY SONS!"** I shout. Zach flashes that irresistible grin. "It's okay, Mom," he laughs. I tap the table with my fist and lower my voice—"These are my sons."

I order the Mediterranean omelet.

Here is a great short memoir by Harriette Ginsberg

Hold On

Mid-August, just two weeks after I turned sixteen, I took my driver's test and passed it. I thought I was hot stuff getting the license on the first try so soon after I had started driving. My parents had only one car, a large blue and white Pontiac. If I wanted to "take the car," I had to drive both of my parents to work in the morning and then pick them up at the end of the work day. I just loved to drive and feel like the self-determined, invincible, and smarter-than-my-poor-parents person I thought I was.

One late afternoon, must have been a Saturday as only my mother was in the car with me, we were cruising down the "expressway" at a pretty good clip. The highway recently had opened in what had been the old subway bed, so it was a big deal to be sailing along on it. I was at the wheel going the full speed limit when the front tire blew and the car went into a heavy shimmy. My mother yelled, "Hold on!" I did and brought the shaking car slowly over to the shoulder of the road, not far from the Culver Road Armory. In my memory, it took only a breath or two before a police car came up and parked behind us. The officer got out of his car and came over to my window. He looked past me and told my mother that he had been on the bridge overhead and seen the whole thing, and that I had done a good job.

Those words never left me. Not the policeman's words, but my mother's. "Hold on" has been what has gotten me through many difficult situations. When I need courage or the feel of someone's hand on my back, I hear my mother saying, "Hold on," and I do.

———— ❧ ————

Note the use of the *flashback* in the next sample. Very nice touch.

Driving down Lake Avenue recently, I was momentarily transported back in time. Holy Sepulchre and Riverside Cemeteries border Lake Avenue just south of the neighborhood in which I grew up. These cemeteries, peaceful, quiet, with winding roads throughout were where our dad took us to begin our driving lessons. He liked teaching us in these out-of-the-way locations because, as he said, "You can't kill anyone here!"

My older brother and I did well during our lessons with dad, but our younger brother was known for daydreaming, even while driving! (I believe this is true even today!) He was off in some thoughtful place, well away from his lesson, when he cornered too swiftly and very nearly wiped out a headstone placed all too close to the bend in the road.

Fortunately he and dad survived and learned to laugh about the experience. As the youngest, he was the last child to be given lessons by dad. I expect that caused dad a certain amount of joy.

⸺⸰⸰⸰⸺

WHERE'S THE KEY?
BY MARCIA LEWIS

My mom on occasion would leave the house without her key. Well, when we got home she opened her purse and there was no key. This happened at least three or four times a year. How did Mom, my sister, and I get into the house?

At the back of the house was a milk box. I was the designated child to wiggle through the milk box. Originally, I think it was my idea. Since the milk box was quite high, my mom opened the box, picked me up, and I was ready to go through the small opening. My body was skinny and wiry and just right for me to crawl through the milk box, and then directly into the cupboard where the canned goods were stored. I'd take the soup cans, the tuna cans, and other varieties of staples and make a narrow aisle to crawl on my belly and finally reach the cupboard door. I opened it gingerly and pulled my body on to a step that would take me directly to the back door.

I was the rescuer of my mom and sister. I happily unlocked the latch and opened the back door smiling and laughing. What an adventure for me, as I looked forward to the next time my mom left the house without her key.

⸺⸰⸰⸰⸺

This Elderwriter piece brought back memories for all of us.

MY PEANUT GALLERY

Buffalo Bob Smith would say, "Kids, what time is it?" The response would be, "It's Howdy Doody time!" The kids in the peanut gallery would sing the theme song and I sang along.

Clarabell, Princess Summerfall Winterspring, and even cranky Phineas T. Bluster were rock stars to the five-year-old me. But I remember always really looking at the peanut gallery—they were my people.

November of 2012, on the occasion of my "Special Birthday," Paul and

Vicki, Lisa, Joe, and the children all gathered to celebrate me. After dinner, my birthday cake was brought out and, lo and behold, there on the cake were Howdy Doody and Buffalo Bob. They remembered.

It made me think that special day of my own peanut gallery—those gone from it by death and distance, but also how lucky I am to fill it now with children, grandchildren, granddogs, and wonderful friends. It really is a Howdy Doody time in my life!

———— ≈≈≈ ————

Elderwriter Mary Connolly wrote several short memoir pieces and called them "Life Lessons." Here is one of them.

After a quick shower I watch as Grandpa squeezes into his clean jeans and a shirt. Excitedly he is getting ready to go to the race track with Donna. She knows the owner of one of the horses running in the eighth race. Both firmly believe that this will give them luck when they bet on him.

Donna appears at our front door. I can tell that she is just as excited as Grandpa. She is dressed in purple from head to toe.

I follow them both down the sidewalk thinking to myself that Donna may just be an angel. I look at her shoulders to see if she has sprouted wings. Angels come in all shapes, sizes, and ages. God hides them in people. When we find out who they are we must keep that secret. If we tell, they fly to some other person.

Life Lesson: Do kind things for others. You never know—they may be an angel.

📁 Content for Very Short Memoir Pieces

In Chapter 1, I presented an overview of PLD content. Short memoir pieces draw heavily on "fond memories" material. Let's review those—family holidays, childhood, rites of passage, military experiences, encounters with nature, sports triumphs, religious or spiritual awakenings, professional accolades, performance events.

Of course, not all memories are fond. You may choose to write about a time when hardship or misfortune forced you to marshal your resources, rise to the occasion, evaluate your priorities, turn your life around. Short memoir pieces based on overcoming adversity can be very powerful.

DATES AND TITLES ON YOUR PIECES

Consider putting a date and title on your short memoir piece. These devices help you communicate with the reader.

Locating the event in time aids the reader's understanding. Sometimes the date *is* the title; sometimes the date is included in the piece.

Titles give the reader a head's up about what's coming. They direct the reader toward a particular interpretation of the piece. Titles allow you to hint at inferences that can be drawn from the piece, but are not spelled out explicitly. Titles are a good thing.

HELPFUL HINTS: SHORT SENTENCES; WHEN IN DOUBT

1. Beginning a short memoir with a very short sentence is an effective way to draw in the reader.

» Friday the 13th was our lucky day.

» Hallelujah!

» Missing you.

» I wasn't used to compliments.

These short sentences are little attention grabbers.

I like the short sentence at the end, too. Ending with a very short sentence allows you to add a personal note without disrupting the flow of the piece.

» She stood me up.

» They're waiting for me.

» I love these guys.

These short sentences aren't punch lines. They're closers.

2. In the words of Daniel Patrick Moynihan, "You are entitled to your own opinions; you are not entitled to your own facts." In creative nonfiction, your reader has the right to assume the facts you have presented are 'true' to the best of your knowledge.

When

» you are in doubt about your facts;

» you want to go beyond your best recollection;

> » you want to describe a representative scene or use a metaphor;

> » you are making a conjecture about your past;

you can alert the reader with lead-ins like:

> » I imagine…

> » In my mind…

> » It may, or may not, be true that…

> » Perhaps…

> » It's just possible that…

> » Is it possible that…?

> » I like to think…

✐ EXERCISE 11. WRITING A VERY SHORT MEMOIR PIECE

Aim to have at least two or three short memoir pieces in your document. Their impact is in their brevity. If your writing takes more than half a page, whittle it down. Use the Memory Retrieval Exercise to recreate the details. Short memoir pieces are a wonderful way to *Celebrate Your Life!*

✐ EXERCISE 12. A TIME CAPSULE

For a little change of pace—try a Time Capsule. Suppose you have a metal box 1ft x 1 ft x 1.5 ft.. As of today, what eight or ten items would you put in the box if you knew it wasn't going to be opened for one hundred years? What indispensable twenty-first century paraphernalia would you drop in there? Keep it light-hearted.

CHAPTER 6

WORDS OF THE HEART

IN CHAPTER 6 YOU WILL:

» consider the importance of poems in legacy writing

» consider writing an occasional poem

» start thinking about epigraph and title

I AM ALWAYS TOUCHED BY THE excitement and pride the Elderwriters feel when they complete their first poem.

POEMS

Here's my observation about poetry: not many people read it. It may have something to do with that high school experience when, no matter how hard you tried, your interpretations weren't quite right. Poetry can be intimidating, frustrating. Our discomfort carries over into the writing of poetry.

Now, here's my observation about Elderwriters—they start out writing prose, but at some point they turn to poetry. Most of us don't think we can write a poem until we do. **Poems** have a special place in personal legacy writing. They are the words of the heart.

Before we get into a fuller discussion of poetry, let's look at some examples from class.

Her husband's memory was failing, so this participant created a collection of short pieces that would allow him to revisit the good times in their marriage again and again. What a wonderful idea!

TENNIS AGAIN

Yesterday we played tennis again,
Last year's injury now a memory.
Probably taking ten seconds off
Retrieving the ball,
But the newly resurfaced court
Made up the difference.

Cancer, financial reversals, a teenager to raise
Didn't defeat you.
We played tennis again,
In the sun by the lake,
Hitting straight and solid,
Just like on our first date
Thirty years ago.

Here is a poem Doris M. Meadows wrote about her husband. She sent a copy to her children on Father's Day.

WINNING THE LOTTERY

It was a trillion dollar jackpot
A ten carat diamond
A billion dollar mansion
Mountains of gold and silver
And all luxury imaginable
All rolled into one.

One man,
Douglas Shelby Meadows,
My soul mate
My best friend
My husband
My intellectual partner
My lover.

Your father.

Pam Erwin writes about a much-loved piano.

BABY GRAND

Gramps and Gram Benham
gave you to me
after having been in
their home for many years.

You were tuned today,
your top left open
inviting me to
let the sound come out.

My fingers are rusty,
aching to produce those
sounds of yesteryears,
together we work.

Your upper harmonies feel thin,
the sound a bit too brilliant,
the lower range still registers
some mellow tones.

After many years of
working for me, my children,
and my many students
it's nearing the time
to say good-bye.

Chris shares the loss of a dear, long-time friend who passed away.

FOR MY DEAR FRIEND, PEGGY

As you are gone
So we are
A piece of us
Has flown afar
Left adrift
Without a star

We lose ourselves
Along with you
The lives we shared
Have changed their hue.
I miss that part of me
No longer there
Because my memories
I cannot share
No one knows
The times we knew
No one knows
And that's the loss
Of Me and You

By Chrissy 2010

Loss is frequently expressed in poems.

CAROL

A bright light entered the room.
    Vivacious, funny, beautiful.
Sensitive, caring and thoughtful.
    She was my soul mate.

A hole is in my heart.
    It will never heal.
The pain will always hurt.
    The missing will never stop.

Poems can also be used to express wonderment and joy.

POEM

What wonderful sights to have seen
The Emerald Isle, shades of green
Galway Bay, the Atlantic shore
Sheep on the hillsides, the Cliffs of Mohr
A stop at a roadside, and all around
A picture postcard could be found

In Connemara in County Galway
A more beautiful place I've not seen to this day
Kylemore Abbey, men gathering turf
To sit by a turf fire, I can't measure its worth
Londonderry and Belfast City
Remembering their histories, oh, such a pity
The murals in Belfast, the high walls in Derry
Gave me cold chills as I walked and I tarried
Thinking of those imprisoned and killed
Fighting for freedom, I remember them still
Many sights remain that need to be seen
In this beautiful isle with shades of green
The dream that I hold is to return
To the land of my ancestors, for this I do yearn.

This is a poem I wrote about my sons.

THESE MEN

Who are these men?
My babies, my boys,
these men.

Grown ups with wives
and separate lives.
Dreams unfurled,
you throw back your shoulders
and meet the world.

Far away, going gray,
you'll always stay -
my babies, my boys,
these men.

Here's one more by Chris written for her mom on her 95th birthday

What could be better
    not a card or a letter
but an heirloom tomato, so juicy and red
    between two slices of homemade bread

It's a gift
    of a sort
on a day of import
    HAPPY 95TH BIRTHDAY, MAMA

Here is a poem one of our Elderwriters composed reflecting on a long period of sadness in her life.

The birds of sorrow
    pass over my head
        I weep and mourn
           My loved ones—dead.
                But as my days
                    become so rare
                        I'll not allow those birds
                            to nest in my hair.

Let's talk about poems.

- » As personal legacy writers, you're not bound by any formal definition of poetry. Whatever works, works. The one inviolable characteristic of poetry is compression. Poems are compact expressions of your thoughts and feelings. They are lean. You can't get in there and ramble. You'll lose your punch.

- » It is a fairly common misconception that poems have to rhyme. They don't. The *right* word is more important than the *rhyming* word.

- » You are free to do whatever you want with punctuation, capitalization, line length, and shape. Unless you're hoping to become the next poet laureate, none of that matters. What matters is that you have said what you wanted to say and made your point.

- » Poems can mourn or celebrate.

- » Poems can be just plain fun.

- » Poems are often the format of choice when we're writing about sad, difficult, or confusing times in our lives—times when we felt vulnerable

- » Rites of passage fit nicely into a poem. Review your table of contents—are there some topics you feel lend themselves to a poetic form?

- » Remember, you can use other peoples' poems to complement your prose pieces.

Consider these types of poems.

» The couplet—2 lines.

> Try a Sudoku?
> Merci beaucoup!

» Haiku—a short poem of Japanese origin—3 lines

5 syllables	Family has gone.
7 syllables	The funeral is over.
5 syllables	I sit here alone.

» Limerick—A humorous, rhyming 5 line poem (AABBA)

> You remember these—There was a young lady from Kent...

» Free Verse—For our purposes, anything goes. What a gift.

» Acrostic—Looked at vertically, the first letter of each line spells a word or phrase. Hands down, the most famous acrostic of all time is the lyrics to a 1915 song by Howard Johnson and Theodore Morse.

> M-O-T-H-E-R
> M is for the million things she gave me
> O means only that she's growing old
>
> .
>
> .
>
> .

Put them all together they spell MOTHER, a word that means the world to me. Everybody knows that one.

Kathleen Toole wrote this very subtle acrostic poem about listening to her mother play the piano. If you look closely, you see that when you put together the first letter of each stanza you get CHOPIN.

> C
> H
> O
> P
> I
> N

NOCTURN Op. 9 #1

Calling upon sounds of childhood
remembering those many times
of just you and me

Hearing music through finger touches
creating music so elegiac
enrapt, I had become
Opening yourself to melodic strains
swaying, so slightly, humming too
I move closer to you

Playing piano, pianissimo-forte!
hands sweep, glide-up and down the keys
Eyes closed, enveloped in sound I sit

Imagining—*What is she thinking?*
Creeping nearer to view you –
Soft, serene, calm

Nothing now can match that time
playing what once I heard from you
remembrances are they now

lovingly so

A memory of Joycie

» Ballads, Hymns, and Prayers

» I want to repeat a couple of sentences from Chapter 1: Personal legacy writing includes selecting a format for each piece that enhances its meaning, tone, and presentation. Varying the written landscape adds depth and richness to your work, gives more options for self-expression, showcases your sense of humor, and draws the attention of the reader.

Poems are a great way to vary the landscape.

THE OCCASIONAL POEM

There is something called an *occasional* poem—a poem written to commemorate a particular occasion.

Here is Janet Nemetz's grand poem written to commemorate her 70th birthday.

BIRTHDAY SONG
janet nemetz

praise
    for arriving at seventy
i plan to be healthy
no diseases for me
i'll wait until eighty
        maybe ninety

no wearing purple
unless it's flattering
toss out
frumpy grumpy
        oldcrow thoughts
it's too late for me
    can't change
        can't help it
           too set in my ways

brain furniture needs changing
scarred   scratched   gnawed
no longer fits
    this house
trade in
for clean   uncluttered   space
to write new memories

this crone will arrive
in cinderella's coach
dancing slippers
bright red   but comfortable

ready
for the rest of the ball

✍ Exercise 13. Write a Poem Using the "Kobylak" Form

Wesley Kobylak has used a flexible format—a combination of prose and poetry lines—in this piece from his chapbook, *Moments*

Memories of You Before You Were Born

When you kids were young babes, you'd scribble, and draw, and color, and create magnificent art—abstract at first, then folk. I could never do it myself, only see it happen. It was frustrating.

> My children scribble so
> Easily why
> Can't I?

When I made your cradle, I had a tough time sanding the bottom evenly.

> Finally
> This board and I
> After cursing each other
> Are straight

And the experience of wood working teaches so much.

> Right-angle carpentry
> Neither this nor that
> But precisely so

When we moved to Tusky, the first thing I fell in love with was the silence. And the cows.

> I never heard the silence
> Until the far off mooing
> reached me

The pattern is: One long sentence, three short phrases. One long sentence, three short phrases.

Very effective. Easy to work with. I used this form for poems in my own document.

Write a poem utilizing the Kobylak form. You may want to start with clustering to gather data for your piece. The long sentences are key. They set the stage for the short phrases. You'll be surprised at how well this works.

✍ ## EXERCISE 14. TRY AN ACROSTIC

Liz Rowsick is the source of several very creative legacy pieces. Read through her acrostic about a treasured visit to her son.

FLORIDA VACATION

From our landing to our
Leaving
Our every moment with you is
Remembered in our hearts.
In the hours and days
Doing what we can together,
Acquiring and creating memories and

Visions to call upon and relive,
Actuality and reality take a needed rest.
Certain that the sweet time we
Anticipated for so long will
Turn all too quickly
Into bittersweet departing,
Our hearts beat in unison to the words…
Not yet, not yet, not yet.

Each line is *not* a complete sentence. The sentences wrap around to the next line. This gives the piece a different feel.

Try your hand at an acrostic. See what you come up with.

📖 ## EPIGRAPHS/EPIGRAMS AND A TITLE FOR YOUR PLD

Keep your eye out for a short poem, song lyrics, quotes, or lines from a book that you feel summarize your outlook on life. An epigraph or epigram right at the beginning of your PLD is a nice touch.

Most of the Elderwriters have put a title on their document. Here are some examples:

» *Just Wanted to Say…*
» *Life is What Happens While You're Letting Out the Dog*
» *Phoenix*
» *I'd Like to Say a Few Words*
» *My Turn*
» *There's Something I'd Like to Say*

CHAPTER 7

THE MANY USES OF LETTERS

IN CHAPTER 7 YOU WILL:

» delve into letters as a legacy writing format

» look at opening letters

» pick up a couple hints

OUR ARSENAL OF PERSONAL LEGACY writing formats is growing. We've highlighted lists—both simple and embellished—sayings and quotations, paragraphs, vignettes, narratives, very short memoirs pieces, and poems. Not bad. In Chapter 7 we deal with letters.

🗐 LETTERS

Letters are familiar—we've all written and read letters. There's nothing daunting about letters. Let me share some thoughts about letters.

» Letters are the perfect vehicle when you have something heartfelt to say to someone. From my pen to your ears—one on one. Participants have written letters of affection, apology, appreciation, and regret. You may write a letter to anyone—past, present, or future; famous or familiar. One Elderwriter wrote a letter to her late husband just to catch him up on what's happened since he passed.

» As with poems, there are *occasional* letters—letters written to commemorate special occasions.

Here is just such a letter.

To Helen on the Occasion of Her Solo Performance in a Musical Revue

February, 2012

Dear Helen,

It *was* a grand night for singing! We were a little concerned at first. Due to director oversight, you were one of the last members of the chorus to appear on stage. Then we spotted you—marching along, arms swinging, head high, belting out the opening song. What a rush!

After a few more numbers, the stage cleared, the lights went down, a lone spotlight shown on a lone singer. The director got it right this time—you were exquisite. Beautiful dress, a rose in your hand, you could have heard a pin drop. I was struck by the deep richness of your voice as you sang "If I Loved You." You brought down the house.

During the intermission, the woman next to us asked if we had family in the cast. Family, indeed. We were there by choice! And so were you, Helen. So were you. You're a model for us all. Too often retirement becomes a spectator sport. Take a risk; get out of your comfort zone; be proactive—you showed us how it's done. It was a privilege to be there to support you. I wouldn't have missed it for the world.

With great fondness and admiration,

Sue

» In Chapter 12 we will look at the Ethical Will—an end-of-life letter to loved ones affirming values and beliefs.

» Give your readers a window on your values. Write a letter to someone famous expressing your admiration or disapproval of his/her actions.

To:
Susan B. Anthony
19 Madison Street
Rochester, New York 14608

Dear Ms. Anthony,

Thank you—from all of us.

Best regards,
The Women of the United States

» Don't forget letters to the editor—short statements of your position on issues of concern. This is your chance to take a stand.

» A friend of mine wrote an op-ed decrying the unwillingness of some drivers to observe the handicapped parking regulations. Good for her. Perhaps you have previously published op-eds. Dust them off and put them in your PLD. (Op-eds are so called because they were located opposite the editorial page. This is a good place to go for examples of short opinion statements.)

» One of our participants used a Dear Abby format to describe a period of dysfunction in her family.

» Another participant wrote an open letter to her congregation imploring them to embrace "the diversity in God's Garden"—an incredibly personal and powerful piece.

» Write a letter you wish you had written.

» Letters may be among the documents in your PLD. When a friend of mine—whose name also happens to be Susan—turned 21, her father wrote her a letter sharing his views about what sort of man he thought she should marry. She didn't get married for another thirty years. Her dad had passed away by then, but she read his letter at her wedding. Here is an excerpt from that letter. Perfect addition to her PLD.

Dear Susan,

You know what you want in a man—you want him to be honest, sincere, loyal, peaceful, happy, and prosperous. You don't want to make him over and neither do you want him to make you over. There has to be mutual freedom and respect.

It is not a true marriage when one marries for money, social position, or lift of ego. This indicates a lack of sincerity, honesty, and true love. A union under these conditions is a sham and a masquerade.

If you don't come up 100% in your heart and mind on these basics, don't despair; repeat to yourself that you will find such a man and you will know it when you see him or meet him.

Love,
Dad

✍ Exercise 15. Writing a Letter for Your PLD

Reread the bullets about letters. Find one that appeals to you and craft a letter. If you don't have any ideas right now, put this on your to-do list and come back to it.

📖 THE OPENING LETTER

Nearly every PLD contains an **opening letter** of some kind. The opening letter may not be written until the rest of your document is finished or it may be something you think about and edit over time. The opening letter identifies your reader(s) and informs them regarding the what and why of your document.

Here are a few samples.

Hello,
This project was done without a specific person or audience in mind.
So…..
Welcome:
To my thoughts,
My views,
My life as I see it.

I hope I surprise you but, if not, I hope you at least find a poem, a thought, or a point of view that you find interesting.

I hope it inspires you to examine your own life, thoughts, and viewpoints and share them.
So, whoever you are; I wish you joy in all that you do…
Rose Booth
2012

————⊗⊗⊗————

I've always believed that we are different
people to different people.
This document was created with love and
affection from thoughts and memories
that I hold dear to my heart.
I hope I've been able to shine a light on
a facet you might not have known was
there. Perhaps a me you've just met.

Chris
2012

————⊗⊗⊗————

May 29, 2012

Dear Dan,

I first need to thank Aunt Kathy for sending "A Grandmother's Journal" to Grandma. That is what led to my decision to write my own story.

There were so many questions in your grandma's journal; some were answered, others left blank, still others left me questioning why, or tell me more. Unfortunately, I didn't read it while Grandma was still alive so the questions will remain unanswered, the stories incomplete.

Writing my story is an ongoing endeavor—to be completed during my lifetime for you to read and, hopefully, treasure.

Written for you with all my love,
Mom

✍ EXERCISE 16. BEGIN WORK ON AN OPENING LETTER

Begin work on an opening letter, even if it's just to set up a folder.

🚂 HELPFUL HINTS: EXISTING FAMILY LETTERS; INCLUDING A SAMPLE OF YOUR HANDWRITING

1. Quite a few Elderwriters have letters that were written between their parents during World War II. They have included one or two of them in their documents.

2. The general consensus is that you should have something in your PLD that is in your own handwriting—even if it is only your signature. I still get a wave of loneliness when I see my parents' signatures. The opening letter is one piece you might consider writing and/or signing in long hand.

Chapter 8

Special Effects

In Chapter 8 you will learn about a variety of special effects you can use in your document.

📖 Special Effects

Let's take a break from the writing and talk about **special effects**.

» The personal computer makes adding special effects to your document easy and fun. You may need a little help from your grandchildren, but if you own a computer, chances are you can achieve these effects.

» If you do not have access to a computer, you can still add special effects to your document, you just have to create them yourself. The good news is you only have to do it once. You can get high-quality copies, on acid-free paper, from your local copy shop.

» Special effects add pizzazz to your document—a ribbon in your bonnet, a flower in your lapel. This is your life. Look sharp.

» Special effects draw the attention of the reader and break up the monotony of continuous text.

» Special effects add supplemental information to your work.

» Special effects show another side of your personality, another side of your creativity.

» Special effects enhance your written work by altering its physical appearance.

» Can special effects be overdone? Yes. Can they detract from the tone and intent of a written piece? They can. Do you have to be judicious in your use of special effects? Absolutely.

Much of what I know about special effects I have learned from the Elderwriters. Here are some things that have been successful.

1. Most of you have Microsoft Word, MacPages, or some other word processing application. You can change the font and size of the print. **Helvetica in size 14.**

2. Webdings and Wingdings—One day Liz Rowsick came into class with a map of all the characters in the Webdings and Wingdings fonts—my life hasn't been the same since. What a gift. Thank you, Liz.

The icons I use to identify sections of most chapters are from these fonts.

Formats… Wingdings 2, . (that's the period), size 16, bold

Content… Wingdings, 1, size 16, bold

Document construction… Wingdings, &, size 16, bold

Helpful Hints… Webdings, h, size 18, bold

To get a copy of the chart of all the characters available in Webdings, Wingdings, Wingdings 2, and Wingdings 3 go to www.speakingppt.com. There will be a blue box in the upper right hand corner that says "Enter search items." Type in "Wingdings Fonts." You will see—"Finally! A printable Character Map of Wingdings Fonts." Click on the word "Printable." The map will appear. You will see the instructions "Click here for a printable version." Click there. The map will fill the screen. Just print it out. Keep it with you at all times.

3. Can you add a photo? You bet. The technology is wonderful.

» Find the photo you want to use.

» Find someone who's done this before to assist you.

Most home printers have a scan feature that will allow you to get the image into your computer. That's the first hurdle. (It's also possible for someone with a scanner to e-mail the image to your computer. Too much information? Truthfully, I don't recommend you try this on your own unless you already have the skills. It can be very frustrating.)

Then once you're in Word or Pages, you can INSERT a picture, make it larger or smaller, rotate it, change the tone, hue, or sharpness—mind-boggling.

If you don't have a computer, or grandchildren, your local copy shop can help.

4. Another image you can INSERT into a text page is Clip Art, which is already stored in your computer. In your word processing program, go to INSERT—PICTURE—CLIP ART. There are also Clip Art images on the Internet that you can access.

5. The Internet is a source of maps, words to songs and poems, and historical information you might need.

6. Elderwriters bring a lifetime of experiences and skills to the PLD process. Unlike myself, many have shown unusual creativity in the use of scrap-booking, rubber stamps, drawing, photography, and book arts. The results have been stunning. Some of these endeavors have been one-of-a-kind productions, others have been successfully duplicated.

7. The foreign language phrase can be effective, particularly if that language is part of your life. One of our participants, born in Bavaria, opened her PLD with a Rilke poem—first in the original German, then the English translation. Very nice.

8. I've seen PLDs with time lines, spread sheets, PowerPoint, and puzzles. A judicious use of these special effects highlights your ingenuity and holds the attention of the reader

9. Sometimes the nature of the piece itself creates a special effect.

Here is another piece by Liz Rowsick .

My October Vagabonds' Geneology

My paternal grandfather was born October 17, 1894.

His son, my uncle, Frank, was born on October 15, 1934.

My husband, Fritz, was born on October 6, 1939.

My oldest son, Ron, was born on October 27, 1968.

His first wife, Debbie, was born on October 20, 1963.

Their son, Cooper, was born on October 5, 1998.

Ron's second wife, Dawn, was born on October 8, 1968.

My youngest son, Matt, was born on October 19, 1971.

His wife, Melissa, was born on October 2, 1968

Their son, Joshua, was born on October 1, 2001

Me? I was born on my Uncle Frank's 13th birthday, October 15, 1947.

10. You can also add boxes, borders, and shading or alter the arrangement of the text.

SMELLS, SMELLS, SMELLS
BY EDWIN KINNEN

What smells do you remember from when you were a little kid? Burning leaves in the Fall? The smoke of a burst firecracker on the 4th of July? Your sweaty uncle when he came home from work and gave you a hug? Three other smells are also stuck in my head.

Grandmother lived with her widowed daughter in an upstairs flat. When we'd go to their house, my sister and I could see in a dim corner a statue of a black boy holding a red berry up over his mouth. A stuffed pheasant looked down at us from the top of a nearby bookshelf. Two large cats would be slinking around the kitchen among potted geraniums on the windowsill. Grandmother was always sitting in her rocker dressed all in black except for her white lace collar. She would give us a hug, pat us on our heads, and then we try to hurry back to our Mother. I remember this because I best remember the smell of the apartment—musty, cattish, and geraniums. Whew.

Dad and Mom drank coffee sometimes, I guess—don't remember. However, I do remember the grocery store in town that sold coffee beans. Our weekly shopping trips to the A&P (Atlantic and Pacific Tea Company) would include a walk down the isle where the store had a machine for grinding coffee beans. The smell of that fresh ground coffee in the A&P was intoxicating.

Being the only boy in the family, it was my Saturday job to collect waste paper and household rubbish to take to the backyard and burn it. I didn't mind this job as I could make a fire and discover all sorts of interesting things that my parents discarded. Often I would also find a few cigar butts from my Dad's Sunday afternoon smoke. As these butts still had about an inch of good cigar, I'd put them on the end of a stick and "smoke" them down to half of an inch. When the wind was just right, the unpleasant smell of smoldering rubbish mixed with cigar smoke imprinted my small brain and I could recognize it again anywhere.

✍ Helpful Hints: Another Plug for Working in a Small Group

I want to reiterate the benefits of being part of a legacy writing group. From my experience with the Elderwriters classes, the whole is greater than the sum of its parts. The collective sharing of ideas and expertise gets everyone's creative juices flowing. Hearing your pieces read aloud builds pride and confidence. The group provides energy and motivation when you get bogged down.

It is not necessary for everyone in the group to be at the same stage of legacy writing. Members with more experience have valuable know-how to contribute, while beginners see the project through a fresh new lens. Personal legacy writing is a celebration. Everybody wins.

✍ Exercise 17. Creating a Virtual Memory Box

What do you save when someone dies? One of our participants put me onto the idea of a Memory Box—a pretty box of manageable size in which you store memorabilia with special meaning for you. Instead of taking food when making a condolence call, this woman sometimes takes a Memory Box—empty except for a poem she has written about the deceased. The family provides the contents.

Your PLD offers you an opportunity to create a Virtual Memory Box for a loved one. Here are the Virtual Memory Boxes I created for my parents. They include items I did save, and a few(*) I wish I had kept, but didn't.

Memory Box for C. Howard Shaffer (1912—2009)	Memory Box for Marcia B. Shaffer (1919—1996)
his death certificate	*her wedding rings*
3 photos: two from his 90th birthday party, one as a physics teacher	*an official paper confirming her date of birth*
*his fishing vest and 3 trout flies	*her obituary*
his last wallet	*her address book*
a letter of commendation from the Buffalo Board of Education upon his retirement in 1972	*the velveteen collar from her Chesterfield coat*
a copy of his article for the Michigan Streamside Journal in 2005 describing his experience as a boy of 10 watching Len Halliday tie an Adam's Fly.	*2 photos: a graduation photo receiving her MA from the University of Buffalo, another taken shortly before she died*
*the two empty shotgun shells he carried in his raincoat pocket so he could identify his London Fog on the coat rack at Ripa's or the Elks	*a poem Zach wrote about going to Hatch Lake with Gram*
the card we handed out at his memorial gathering on September 26, 2009	*a copy of the article she wrote for the Journal of School Psychology in 1984*

Create a Virtual Memory Box for someone and include it in your PLD.

Sample **Build-A-Page** — a potpourri of writings on a single topic.

MY AGE PAGE

3 favorite age quotes:

I don't think about my age. I think about my time—and my time is now.
- Albert Finney on turning 70

I do not wish to achieve immortality through my works. I wish to achieve immortality by not dying.
- Woody Allen

I'm beginning to feel like an old man.
- My dad on turning 95

GETTING OLDER

Citracal and Ocuvite
Metamucil, what a fright.
Pension's shrinking, hair's receding
Ohmygod, my gums are bleeding.
Body's crumbling, husband snores
But through it all my spirit soars.
You ask me why I feel so gay?
My Social Security check arrived today.

☺

☞ RULES FOR OLD WOMEN AND OLD MEN

1. Don't procrastinate. Set deadlines.
2. Floss.
3. Stay connected with young people.
4. Get out of your comfort zone occasionally.
5. Keep learning new things.
6. Don't send checks to television evangelists.
7. Don't buy anything you can't take to assisted living.
8. Get used to being invisible.
9. Walk, walk, walk.
10. Enjoy the beauty of the planet.
11. Set up a prepaid funeral and burial.
12. Help others.

INTERVIEW AT THE GATE

A short one-act play for two voices.

With cautious optimism, I approach St. Peter.

Have you always loved the Lord your God
with all your heart and soul and mind?   Probably not.

Have you always lived by the Ten Commandments?   Probably not.

Have you consistently given of your time, talent,
and money to those less fortunate?   Probably not.

Do you have any questions?   Will I get in?

Probably not.

SURVIVOR GUILT

I'm part of a swath of the U.S. population that has consistently been at the
right place at the right time. We are roughly 65—72 years old.

Too young for the Depression, WW II, and Korea, we enjoyed the subsequent
economic growth and development of our nation.

We were not held accountable for industrial waste and environmental
damage. Those debts will be paid by future generations.

Our sons and daughters were not drafted.

We are the beneficiaries of the great strides in medical and dental science.

We were the first to have the pill, reproductive rights, the elastic waist. Right
on time—just as if we had ordered them up.

Our federal entitlements are secure—we're grandfathered in.

No one can match our pensions.

Luck. Dumb luck.

We owe.

Sue Barocas announces the arrival of her first

Dental Implant

Please join us to celebrate this event.

There will be a special appearance by the

Tooth Fairy

who will leave a check for $3000 under Sue's pillow.

✍ EXERCISE 18. BUILD-A-PAGE

My Age Page is a work in progress. Try creating a specialty page of your own.

Look over the Basic Themes and Special Topics list. Highlight a topic you think might be the focus of a page in your PLD. Set up a manila folder for the page.

» Brainstorm the topic using the clustering technique.

» Gather up any sayings or quotes by others you might want to use.

» As we cover additional formats, revisit your topic and experiment with new ways to collect your thoughts and share your feelings.

» Try using different fonts to highlight the various components of your page.

CHAPTER 9

PIECES ABOUT YOUR PAST

IN CHAPTER 9 YOU WILL:

» explore the Family History Piece and the Personal Legacy Essay formats

» consider using stuff as a subject for one or two pieces

» think about the leave-it- in/take-it-out issue

SOME OF THE FORMATS WE consider are standard fare of the writing community—paragraphs, vignettes, narratives, and poems. They are easily defined and well documented. Other formats do not have a formal name, but recur again and again in our legacy writing classes. They describe pieces the Elderwriters have actually written—the embellished list, the very short memoir piece. We're going to look at two more of these novelty, or hybrid, formats in this chapter.

THE FAMILY HISTORY PIECE

The **family history piece** is not a memoir, not an essay, not really a narrative. Running one to two pages, it is simply a description of family history before the writer's time. You might call it an embellished family tree. The piece is devoid of analysis or interpretation. Just the facts, ma'am. The family history piece provides background information and documents events that might otherwise be lost to future generations.

My own family history piece is notable by its absence. Not all families have a robust history that is handed down from generation to generation. I wish I knew more.

✍ EXERCISE 19. WRITING A FAMILY HISTORY PIECE

The family history piece is an excellent inclusion in your PLD. If you have the information, give it a go!

🗐 THE PERSONAL LEGACY ESSAY

A personal essay always involves the author's analysis or interpretation of an issue or event. What I call the **personal legacy essay** is a re-examination and reinterpretation of conditions in our past. Unlike the very short memoir piece that focuses on a specific incident or event, the personal legacy essay is a lookback at the family infrastructure of our formative years and its role in the person we have become. The pieces are short—usually one page or less—and contain insights that may have surfaced as part of the legacy writing process. Legacy writing supports introspection. We make observations and connections we had never thought of before. The passage of time, and your PLD project, help you make sense of your life.

Here is a personal legacy essay by Bonnie Turchetti.

THE UP SIDE OF DOWN

Our family was different. I mean really different. And these differences had a profound impact on our lives.

What separated my family from other families were deaf parents, being Italian *and* Protestant, being raised by a single parent, and poverty.

I could talk about the ways these hurt and caused pain. Instead let me tell you how they gave meaning and quality to my life.

Having deaf parents gave me a sense of value and usefulness that accelerated my maturity. I understood very early that I could help and be proud of myself because I did. I understood what it meant to be able to hear when others may not have been aware of the condition of deafness at all. The sound of my children's voices, whispers in the dark, a bird calling out, a neighbor's hello.

Being Italian and Protestant was sure to get attention. Since I wasn't responsible for either, I was sometimes embarrassed and sometimes amused. Although I was baptized in the Methodist church, it wasn't until I turned 12 that my grandmother hauled me off to Sunday School at the Baptist church. (It's a dangerous time, puberty.) And it was there for a few years that I enjoyed the fellowship of some other Protestant Italian young people. I know the experience shaped much of my thinking. I will always remember the sheer joy of singing hymns, the comfort of the words, and the community of the congregation. Grandma was wise to insist.

By the time I was 10, Dad was gone for good. Hard to imagine an upside to this except to say we did not live with any parental tension. I have seen enough of turmoil in homes to know that the effects can be devastating. Mom was all ours and we were hers for all of her 99 years.

I believe that poverty, if you live through it, is the absolute greatest gift of all. Here is a partial list of things I am so grateful for because I know life without them.

A home of my own
A thermostat to raise in winter
A tree–shaded patio for summer morning coffee
Two bathrooms
Good shoes
Socks without holes
Warm winter coats
Music heard, music played

And one by Elderwriter Doris M. Meadows.

HAPPY MEMORIES

We all have had challenges, difficulties, and downright tragedies as well as happy times, precious occasions, and moments of sheer joy. My family's Scottish stoicism, Irish endurance, and Swiss neutrality emphasized survival rather than success and happiness. My parents primary (but not only) goal was to save and protect us in their survival mode. They had survived depression and war and those dark clouds often overshadowed fun and games.

I remember a conversation between my father and his brother, Uncle Riley, who always slipped us extra ride money for our annual trip to the Amusement Park at Seaside Heights. I think my father knew about the extra money and challenged my Uncle, who said: "Bob, a parent's job is to give their children happy memories." My father responded that a parent had to be strict to make their children strong so when the world knocks them down they will be prepared.

I always valued the good memories approach and I am putting them front and center because they need to be emphasized and nurtured ALWAYS, especially in a family hardwired for survival.

Happy Memories (ages 0-7)
1. Listening to the radio on the rug in the living room while my father smoked a cigar.
2. Looking at my sister's big green Mother Goose book and wishing I could read.
3. Playing in the sun porch on Berkeley Avenue.
4. Having my Aunt Kay McGuire (my mother's best friend) live with us before Roberta was born.
5. Holiday turkey dinners at Nana Will's next door at the kids' table in the kitchen.
6. Visiting and rocking with Aunt BeeBee next door.
7. Mother greeting us at the breakfast table with a chorus of "Smile, darn you. Smile."
8. The sound of the clothes washer in the kitchen and mother humming.
9. Dad cooking Sunday breakfast.
10. Mom serving oatmeal, cream of wheat, Wheatena, or one of her many soups or stews.

In 1984, my mother, Marcia B. Shaffer, was invited to contribute her bio to the *Journal of School Psychology*. The following excerpt is exactly the sort of analysis we're looking for in the personal legacy essay.

One of the dominant influences in my life was the dedication of my family to the Methodist church. My mother was a mainstay of the choir, my father was the church treasurer; we spent all day Sunday and two or three evenings a week among the faithful. The result was a child who was firmly convinced that, to save her own soul, she had to save the world. Once launched on a professional career, I found the good sense to relinquish that unreachable goal, but remnants of it creep into my work at times. It is the kind of moralistic fervor against which one must be eternally on guard.

I was graduated from high school in 1936, in the midst of the Great Depression. We were not rich, but neither were we hungry. My dad always had a job; in fact he was promoted a time or two in the decade of the 1930s. He and my mother were believers in education. Having very little of it themselves, they harbored the illusion that educated people live fuller lives and solve problems more adequately than the untutored. Furthermore, they believed in education for *girls*.

Ours was a typical middle-class home. Oversimplified, men were breadwinners, women were homemakers. I have never felt oppressed by that socially defined role, because it was tacitly assumed, in our family, that one might also have other interests and other achievements if one chose. Being secure in one's role instills a certain amount of self-confidence. Some women's libbers seem to have missed the main point: Eschewing responsibility (such as homemaking) is not necessarily liberating. Unless one has another role to assume, the loss of a stereotype can be confusing. At any rate, no one ever made me feel inferior because I was a girl. I've always thought that when someone said "mankind," I was included.

✍ EXERCISE 20. WRITING A PERSONAL LEGACY ESSAY

The personal legacy essay provides an important link between you and your childhood—a link your descendents will not understand or appreciate unless you tell them. Make this essay a priority. You will be glad you did.

Consider some demographic that impacted your family or set it apart from others in your community—ethnicity, religious affiliation, economic status, number of siblings, language, profession, illness, height/weight, quirks. How did that situation affect your childhood and contribute to your personality/philosophy today? Start crafting a personal legacy essay to include in your PLD.

🗁 STUFF

Stuff is personal. It's *your* stuff. It's much more valuable to you than to the rest of the world. *Legacy stuff* is all those items loved ones have left behind—that hold your memories and force you to cherish and remember. Items like these:

1. Collections
2. Family heirlooms
3. Religious items/ Bible
4. Holiday items
5. Books
6. Military awards or service medals
7. Artwork
8. Dishes

9. Jewelry

10. Recipes

11. Other writings

12. Furniture/ antiques

13. Old toys

14. Photos

15. Quilts

16. Buttons

17. Other treasures

There are stories in stuff. Many wonderful pieces are based on family heirlooms or other items that bring back special memories—legacy stuff. Here is Mary Palmer's very special composition.

My Dad's Secretary Desk

The dark cherry desk, stately as a British butler,
    salutes all who enter our home.
Its broad drawers sit on carved feet
    providing firm support for the pull-down writing surface.
The glass front bookcase holds a selection of poetry books,
    a small assortment of antique milk pitchers, three porcelain birds,
    and a crystal Waterford vase.

How can such an imposing piece of furniture bring me comfort—make me feel secure –
    and warm my heart?

This was my father's desk and the emotions it stirs are the ones my father surrounded me with –
    comfort, security, and loving warmth.

This was where he sat for an hour or two each Sunday,
    checking the accounts, paying bills, and planning the family budget.

Whenever I pass the desk I picture him bent over a pile of papers,
    envelopes, stamps, and his checkbook.

His glasses are on and his tie is loosened. His shirt sleeves are rolled up. There's a cigarette in one hand, a pen in the other, an ashtray and cup of coffee at the top right—just in front of the secret cubby holes.

Walking by I could breathe in the pungent odor of the oil of wintergreen he frequently rubbed on the tense muscles at the back of his neck.

After Dad died, Mom asked me if I wanted the desk. It reminded her too much of him; she cried every time she looked at it.

But I was glad to have it. It doesn't move me to tears. Just the opposite. Dad's secretary desk brings back to me that wonderful sense of security that came from knowing that I was loved and cared for. It makes my dad's presence real—so, even today, I can still feel his love surrounding me.

Piggy-backing on Mary's idea, I wrote this short stuff piece:

My Mom's Chesterfield Coat

My mom bought a new overcoat shortly before she died—a long, black tweed Chesterfield from L.L.Bean—armor against the harsh Buffalo winters. She didn't have a chance to wear it.

After the funeral, I took it home and put it in my closet—seemed a shame to give away a brand new coat. Rochester has bad winters, too.

I love that coat—it *is* my mom. The first time I put it on I knew she was there wrapped around me, keeping me safe. I wear it every winter. In the warm weather, I occasionally reach in the closet and touch the collar, run my hand down the sleeve. I've replaced the buttons and the lining—but it's still Mom keeping me warm.

Gwen Tucker has written a stuff piece based on a family recipe.—great idea!

Coconut Cream Pie On Sunday Morning

Nan baked pies on Sunday morning. She could bake on any day—and often did—but Sunday was the day when she baked early in the morning before we went to church, before we even got out of bed. It was as much a part of Sunday morning as going to Sunday school.

All her pies were "from scratch", everything prepared by her. Of course, there were few pre-cooked pie ingredients back then, but she wouldn't have used them. She'd baked pies for so long that she didn't think about what she was doing; she just made pies. Mixed, assembled, and baked.

It was the scent of the various pies that I remember so well. She made apple, of course, but also, mince, pumpkin, and coconut cream. Coconut cream smelled differently from the others—not as spicy, but smoother. I didn't like coconut cream (there was that texture problem), but somehow managed to eat some of the coconut custard before it went into the pie shell.

Here's Nan's recipe for Coconut Cream Pie. Of course, she never wrote down her recipe, but this one seems closest to hers.

Coconut Cream Pie
1 C. flaked coconut, divided
3 C. whole milk
2 eggs, beaten
¾ C. white sugar
½ C. flour
¼ t. salt
1 t. vanilla extract

1 9" pie shell, baked
(Nan would have prepared this from scratch also.)

1. Preheat oven to 350°.
2. In a medium saucepan, combine milk, eggs, sugar, flour, and salt.
Bring to a slow boil over low heat, stirring constantly.
3. Remove pan from heat and stir in ¾ C. of coconut and the vanilla.
Reserve remaining coconut for top of pie.
4. Pour filling into pie shell and chill till firm, about four hours (it will be ready after morning church services.).
5. Top with remaining coconut and serve.

I seem to remember that Nan put the pie in the oven to brown the coconut on top, but she wouldn't have cooked a cream pie twice. Perhaps she browned the coconut before topping the pie with it.

✍ EXERCISE 21. TRYING YOUR HAND AT A STUFF PIECE

Try your hand at composing a stuff piece. One of our participants wrote several pieces about rings in her family. She called the collection *Rings and Things*. Your stuff piece might be in the form of a poem or letter. Recall Pam Erwin's poem about her piano in Chapter 6. Start with the object and see where it takes you. Good luck!

⬤ HELPFUL HINTS: LEAVE IT IN/TAKE IT OUT

Here's the problem. We're not following a well-beaten path. If we were, there would be PLDs on people's bookshelves and in their safe deposit boxes. You are starting a new tradition for your family. What are the rules?

Only two:

1. Be as truthful and accurate as possible.
2. Don't be hurtful.

Beyond that, are there other guidelines for whether or not to include a piece?

- » A rule of thumb that often serves us well is if you have any concerns, leave it out—the mere fact of questioning a piece is reason to strike it.

- » On the other hand, the writing group usually supports the inclusion of any subject that impacted your growth as an individual or contributed significantly to your becoming the person you are today. Most families—and I dare say, individuals– are touched in some way by substance abuse, physical or psychological abuse, indiscretion, encounters with the law. *How* you handle these issues will be more important that *if* you handle them.

- » After listening to other group members reading warm, uplifting selections about their families, one Elderwriter commented, "It's hard for me to do that. There have been a lot of struggles in my life." What you do, or do not, include in your PLD is your decision. Good struggles lead to new levels of maturity and understanding. Bad struggles pull you down, leave you drained and bitter. Which of your struggles had a lasting effect and which were just a bad patch? How do you want to be remembered?

Certainly, you don't want to appear to be whining. Think about packaging all the negatives in one piece—possibly a poem—and then move on.

Chapter 10

Tell Them Who You Are

QUOTE OF THE DAY:

> Writing is easy; all you do is sit staring at a blank sheet of
> paper until drops of blood form on your forehead.
> —GENE FOWLER

THIS IS THE POINT IN our guide where I break out the pom-poms and go into cheerleader mode. They won't know who you are unless you tell them. Let the horns blow; let the drums roll. This is *your* chance to make a statement. You're on!

THE SHORT PERSONAL ESSAY/PERSONAL STATEMENT

The **short personal essay/personal statement** format puts the spotlight on *you.* What are you passionate about? Golf? Shakespeare? The Argentine tango?

What matters? Education? Politics? Religion?

How do you feel about the direction your world has taken in the last fifty years? How have your opinions on women's issues, technology, or the media changed in that time?

What position have you taken on important issues of the day—world health, the Arab Spring, global warming?

Whoa! Too much information. We don't ruminate about all the issues all the time, but most of us have a few topics of particular interest.

» Topics we pay special attention to in the news, talk shows, family discussions.

» Topics we have wrestled with over the years while trying to arrive at a thoughtful, fair, and consistent position.

» Topics that have moved us to take action, write letters, speak out.

» Topics that have taken us beyond ourselves into the realm of concerned, responsible citizens.

Those are the topics we're looking for.

The short personal essay/personal statement always involves the author's analysis or interpretation of an issue or event. It may be an in-depth look at one topic or a collection of three or four paragraphs, each with a different focus. These are defining pieces—often surprising your family and friends. They may have been completely unaware of your interest and concern.

As always, although I encourage you to adhere to the spirit of the essay, there is no need to be a stickler for form. An opening paragraph, three supporting paragraphs, and a conclusion are not the law. Just tell 'em what you want to tell 'em.

This is a two-part essay I wrote on the military.

THE MILITARY

I.

I confess that I was part of the 1970s anti-military movement. I supported the removal of military recruiting from the public schools, welcomed the end of the draft, and was generally hostile toward the military establishment. Thirty years later—with my sons well beyond conscription age, of course—I feel differently.

First of all, I would require recruitment in the public schools a) Military service is a viable stepping stone to education, training, and personal discipline—for some youth, the only stepping stone. There is considerable evidence that many teens are unaware of the requirements for acceptance into the military. They take paths that preclude participating in the volunteer army and reaping its benefits. b) One could argue against public school recruitment because of the dangers of military service or the level of indoctrination or the disproportionate number of disadvantaged youth who might be put in harm's way. My position: Disadvantaged youth—rural and urban—are already in harm's way. c) I have become an advocate for patriotism. Public school recruitment would expose students to the tremendous pride that exists in the military.

II.

I have a concern about the volunteer army. Around 2005, the media reported several friendly fire and civilian-related incidents. Would a volunteer army attract/accept a higher number of psychologically marginal individuals than a conscripted army?

a) Who decides to volunteer? How many of them have exhausted other employment opportunities because of questionable behavior? I visited one of our local recruiting stations to find out what sort of psychological testing they do—essentially none!

b) A second condition that might contribute to an "instability bulge" in the ranks is periods when the army needs more volunteers. Presumably, the way to attract volunteers is to increase incentives or lower standards.

c) By all reports, the current practice of requiring multiple tours of duty is taking sound soldiers and making them crazy.

Here is Bonnie Turchetti's stunning essay about her cello.

Playing The Cello Is Not For Sissies

The cello is an elegant instrument. At 69, I decided I might be ready to take the challenge and begin to study how to play it. This seemed to be the perfect time in my life. The many years of struggle as a woman, inspired by Betty Friedan, Gloria Steinem, Hillary Clinton, Geraldine Ferraro, and many others, helped me to straighten my backbone so that I can sit tall with poised bow and begin the process.

The *body* of the cello is lovely to look at and touch. I hold it in the crook of my arm and on my breast as I once held other beautiful bodies, which have since outgrown me. They have gone on to add their melodies to the world's chorus.

The elegant graceful *neck* on which is perched the shapely *scroll* reminds me that I too can hold my head erect and enjoy whatever life has to offer. I can see more clearly what is there and how to assess its value to me. Age is so liberating.

The four tightened *strings* are ready to sing out.

The "A" string can express the tripping dance steps of my one-year-old, haltingly running across the room.

The "D" string often carries the theme. My personal philosophy, my beliefs, my joys can so often be reflected in notes on this string. The best of what I have to give is often found here.

The "G" string is lower. This is a no-nonsense string. I can use it to express the opinions I have spent a lifetime thinking about. I can express irritation, anger, or discontent. Where the "D" string may be used to gracefully bring you to my view, the "G" string will emphasize the intensity of my feelings. You may also be brought to exquisite heights of rapture through the full, robust, and mellow sounds. Mood, events, and circumstances may determine how the string is played.

The "C" string: I speak to you through the "C" string; you may look for serious, thoughtful, perhaps dark messages. This is the thickest, toughest, and most difficult string for me to master. It is also the hardest attitude for me to express. I am always disturbed by the heavy-handed, bellicose, and forceful people who use their physicality, money, or power to impose on others. This string also demonstrates the inevitability of conditions we all must face; those conditions we are powerless to control. The tones are deep, but they are not all the same. This string has the same notes as all the others. It's our choice as to how and which we will listen to.

At the bottom of the cello is the *end pin*. Its purpose is to support the body of the instrument. It is always necessary but never provides full support. I often remind myself that the same is true of parenthood. Balance is key.

Each string has a *tuning peg*. Getting out of tune happens frequently and reminds me that when problems arise or I'm out of sorts, I need to listen carefully, think about the problem, and make the proper adjustment. Listening is key.

The master of the music, the object that gives nuance and articulation to the piece, is the *bow*. The pressure or lightness, the long or short, so we hop across the strings or take long sweeping strokes. We can dance across the "A" string, develop and live our philosophies on "D," fight for causes and be a courageous voice for what we believe in on "G." And our "C" string can be a force for good. We can draw strength, benefit from challenges, and accept what we can't change by knowing we have choices in how we use it.

Our lives and relationships are shaped by the use of our personal bow. Learning to use it well, we can enjoy music together; you with your grand opus, me with mine.

This is a piece by Liz Brown. It tells her reader a great deal about her in very few words.

My -ist List

In 1972, I went to my first professional conference—the National School Public Relations Association, in St. Louis. My first plane ride. I was 30 years old.

For a job-alike group (big city school PR people), members were asked to provide a self-description. Here's what I wrote:

"I am a knee-jerk bleeding-heart peacenik liberal, feminist, integrationist, environmentalist, and urban chauvinist."

Almost 40 years later, I still am.

A personal statement can also take the form of a poem. Here is Elderwriter Mary Connolly's poetic statement.

Understanding

You don't seem to understand me
Because you have never been my age
I thought that you knew that I am a bit sluggish
And at a different stage

Yes, I do try to keep up
I just don't seem to know how
I remember when I could
It was at the age that you are now

✍ Exercise 22. Writing a Personal Essay

Every PLD should contain at least one personal essay type piece. Find your topic, then find your voice. Revisit the Basic Themes and Special Topics chart in Chapter 1 for ideas.

✍ Exercise 23. Writing about an Area in Which You Excel

Identify an area in which you excel. Is this a natural talent or something you have cultivated through study and hard work? Discuss how this expertise makes you feel. How has it added to the overall quality of your life?

🗁 The Impact of Historical Events on Your Life

1. Historical events and movements provide a backdrop for the decision-making points in our lives, They may limit, or expand, our options, impact our perceptions, and motivate our choices. Putting your life's milestones in their historical context will add depth and clarity to your work. Here is the opening statement from my Professional Life page.

> I wholeheartedly bought into LBJ's War on Poverty. Education was the answer. Urban teaching was the path to take. From 1975—2001, I approached the teaching of high school mathematics at Wilson Magnet High School with something akin to missionary zeal.
>
> I did not make a difference. If anything, the African American academic situation was worse when I retired than when I began, because hope was dwindling. African American underachievement remains an insoluble problem. It is arguably this nation's most tragic failure.

2. Where were you when:

» they announced the bombing of Pearl Harbor?

» you learned President Kennedy had been shot?

» the Twin Towers were attacked?

Elderwriters have used the personal essay, embellished list, and poems to describe the impact of historical events on their lives and personal philosophies.

Rose Booth shares her reactions to events through the years:

> The first president I remember was President Eisenhower, elected for his second term in 1956; I was 10. I remember the election buttons saying *I like Ike* and that his opponent was Adlai Stevenson. I knew nothing about politics or the issues but 'Ike' had a nifty button and I wore mine proudly. Ah, the power of advertising.
>
> In 1960, U2 pilot Gary Powers's plane was shot down over the USSR while on a US spy mission. I was 13 and totally shocked! I truly believed that the awful Russians spied on us but we AMERICANS WOULD NEVER STOOP SO LOW! I really felt embarrassed for America and I would never view my government with the same innocence. Ah, the power of propaganda.
>
> It was 1963; I was 17 and in my retail class. I was bored and watching the clock when all of a sudden the PA system came on with the announcement

that President Kennedy had been fatally shot while in a Dallas motorcade. We were told to proceed to homeroom and to go home. I went numb...people around me were crying and hugging each other...but I remained numb.

My only thought was: *What will happen to my country now?* Ah, the power that one person can have.

It was July 20, 1969 and I was 23. I was working as an accounts payable clerk for a soda/beer distributor. I had my own apartment and my own car—life was good! And Neil Armstrong walked on the moon! They landed at 9:32 but it was a few hours before they opened the hatch and Neil Armstrong stepped onto the moon's surface. I was thrilled when Mr. Armstrong said: "That's one small step for man, one giant leap for Mankind." Then he plunked down the American flag and I realized that "mankind" was only for "Americans" and this realization made me sad. Ah, the conflict between words and actions.

It was September 11, 2001. I was 55 and at work when the first plane hit the World Trade Center. Our department clerk had been in the break room with the television on and quickly alerted us to the situation. With disbelief I crowded into the room with my co-workers. And then the second plane flew into the second tower, quickly followed by a third plane crashing into the Pentagon. I went into my office, closed the door, and on my knees prayed. Oh my, the power of religion.

Gwen Tucker shares her perspective on changes in ethnic nomenclature.

ETHNICITY

my evolution to African-American

I've been—
  Colored,
  Kline schwartze madchen,
  Negro,
  Black,
  African-American

Never colored, Mama said.
She saw the verb, not the adjective.
Nobody colored us; God made us this way.

We were Negro—more refined, with Spanish roots, and it didn't sound so harsh—she thought.
Mama said we were Negro.

Old man Ehrlich, with his German accent, spoke in his language.
    We ignored those words—he called us all that.
    Besides, I knew I was Negro.

We never replied to the "N" word; we knew the speakers were just the stupid ones.

60s and 70s, college and family.
    Afros, cornrows, dashikis;
    The rise of Black power; fists in salute.
    We were immersed in Blackness.
    I was Black.

Then came African-American.
    What's wrong with Black, I wondered?
    If there's white, why not Black?
    I resisted—it was unnecessary; Black still identified me.

But I relented.
    It was time, it was OK, it was right.
    I am African-American.

3. The Internet is a seemingly endless source of information. You can Google historical events/1960s and get a variety of responses. I have included lists of events from the '60s and '70s to jog your memory.

Historical Events—1960s

1960
1. Alfred Hitchcock's *Psycho* Released
2. First Televised Presidential Debates
3. Lasers Invented
1961
2. Bay of Pigs Invasion
3. Berlin Wall Built
4. Peace Corps Founded

5. Soviets Launch First Man in Space

1962

1. Andy Warhol Exhibits His Campbell's Soup Can

2. Cuban Missile Crisis

3. Marilyn Monroe Found Dead

4. Rachel Carson Publishes *Silent Spring*

1963

1. Betty Friedan Publishes *The Feminine Mistique*

2. President John F. Kennedy Assassinated

3. Martin Luther King Jr. Makes His "I Have a Dream" Speech

1964

1. Beatles Become Popular in U.S.

2. Cassius Clay Becomes World Heavyweight Champion

3. Civil Rights Act Passes in U.S.

4. Nelson Mandela Sentenced to Life in Prison

5. Warren Report on John F. Kennedy's Assassination Issued

1965

1. Los Angeles Riots

2. Malcolm X Assassinated

3. New York City Great Blackout

4. U.S. Sends Troops to Vietnam

1966

1. Black Panther Party Established

2. Mao Zedong Launches the Cultural Revolution in China

3. Mass Draft Protests in U.S.

4. *Star Trek* TV Series Airs

1967

1. First Heart Transplant

2. First Super Bowl

3. Six-Day War in the Middle East

1968

1. Martin Luther King Jr. Assassinated

2. My Lai Massacre

3. Robert F. Kennedy Assassinated

4. Tet Offensive

1969

1. Charles Manson and "Family" Arrested

2. Neil Armstrong Becomes the First Man on the Moon

3. Rock-and-Roll Concert at Woodstock

4. Senator Edward Kennedy Leaves the Scene of an Accident

5. *Sesame Street* First Airs

Historical Events—1970s

1970

1. Beatles Break Up

2. Computer Floppy Disks Introduced

3. Kent State Shootings

1971

1. London Bridge Brought to the U.S.

2. VCRs Introduced

1972

1. M*A*S*H TV Show Premiers

2. Mark Spitz Wins Seven Gold Medals

3. Pocket Calculators Introduced

4. Terrorists Attack at the Olympic Games in Munich

5. Watergate Scandal Begins

1973

1. Abortion Legalized in U.S.

2. U.S. Pulls Out of Vietnam

3. U.S. Vice President Spiro Agnew Resigns

1974

1. Mikhail Baryshnikov Defects

2. U.S. President Richard Nixon Resigns

1975

1. Arthur Ashe First Black Man to Win Wimbledon

2. Civil War in Lebanon

3. Microsoft Founded

1976

1. Nadia Comaneci Given Seven Perfect Tens at Olympics

2. North and South Vietnam Join to Form the Socialist Republic of Vietnam

1977

1. Elvis Found Dead

2. Miniseries *Roots* Airs

3. South African Antiapartheid Leader Steve Biko Tortured to Death

4. *Star Wars* Movie Released

1978

1. First TestTube Baby Born

2. John Paul II Becomes Pope

3. Jonestown Massacre

1979

1. Ayatollah Khomeini Returns as Leader of Iran

2. Iran Takes American Hostages in Tehran

3. Margaret Thatcher First Woman Prime Minister of Great Britain

4. Mother Teresa Awarded the Nobel Peace Prize

5. Nuclear Accident at Three Mile Island

6. Sony Introduces the Walkman

4. You may also want to reexamine, analyze, and share events in your personal history that dramatically impacted your life:

- » a serious illness or accident
- » a natural disaster
- » a spiritual or religious awakening
- » a military involvement
- » a chance encounter

These, too, are defining moments.

✐ EXERCISE 24. WRITING ABOUT A LIFE-CHANGING EXPERIENCE

Have you, or someone in your family, had to deal with a life-changing experience? Write a piece—or a collage of pieces—that share the facts, reactions, and reflections on the situation.

🚚 HELPFUL HINTS: REDUCING THE MONOTONY OF YOUR WRITING

Very short pieces aren't long enough to become monotonous. On the other hand, a one-to-two page narrative or essay may require a little tweaking to hold the attention of the reader. Here are a few suggestions.

- » Vary the length of your sentences. Count the number of words in each sentence of a paragraph. If they're all about the same, try making some of them longer or shorter.
- » Vary the type of sentence. Throw in a question or exclamation once in a while.
- » Include the occasional short dialogue or monologue.

» Feel free to interject personal musings into a piece, as a sidebar or italicized comment. Whisper in the reader's ear.

» Use fragments for emphasis. I. Hate. Broccoli.

» Work on your verbs. The action words you choose make a big difference.

» Dig deeper. Include personal insights.

» Change perspective—try writing from the point of view of the family pet or yourself as a five-year-old. Put a narrative in the present tense.

» Consider a flashback approach where you go from the present to the past then back to the present.

» Include as many sensory details as possible—color, sound, facial expressions, feelings.

» Add photos or clip art.

CHAPTER 11

A FEW MORE WRITING OPTIONS

IN CHAPTER 11 YOU WILL:

» look at several formats—interviews/Q and A, anecdotes, dialogues, one-liners, and micro memoirs

» get information about the printing and preservation of your PLD

I F YOU'VE GOTTEN THIS FAR, you're doing fine. Ever onward.

THE INTERVIEW/Q AND A FORMAT

There are a number of advantages to the **interview/question and answer format**.

» Many of our participants have asked their children if they have any questions/issues they would like to see addressed in the PLD. Why not just include a section with their questions and your answers? Simple enough!

» The interview/Q and A is a great way to deal with odds and ends about your life and intellectual landscape that haven't yet found their way into your writing—items you would like to put out there that haven't fit into any category so far or do not contain enough material to support an essay. The interview/Q and A allows you to cobble together seemingly—or actually—unrelated topics under one heading.

» Readers gravitate toward Q and A—they're fun to read.

» Check out *Life Review* on the internet—you will find a vast collection of prompts and questions. Linda Spence's book, *Legacy: a Step-by-Step Guide to Writing Personal History* also contains prompts and questions that could form the basis of a Q and A piece.

✍ EXERCISE 25.—PEOPLE WON'T KNOW THE REAL YOU UNLESS YOU TELL THEM

Interviews are usually in Q and A form. *Esquire* magazine does an interesting thing with their interviews of famous people. You never see the questions. What appears in the magazine (and online at www.esquire.com/features/what-ive-learned) are the one to five sentence answers, separated by a couple blank lines, presented as a personal statement. The entire interview is one or two pages long. The theme is always some variation on "what I've learned."

Here is Wesley Kobylak's version of the *Esquire* interview.

THINGS I'VE LEARNED: WORDS OF WISDOM

(a la *Esquire*)

I've had some fantastic experiences. You do things and while it's still happening, you say, *Wow, I'm gonna remember this.* Forty, fifty years later, you still remember every detail.

My generation is the post-war generation, the baby-boom. My parents' was the Great Generation, the Depression War. I grew up hearing stories and music from the generation before. You, too. From them to me to you. Everyone has their own generation. It's important to know what that means to you.

The first record I ever asked my mom to buy me was *You Ain't Nothing But a Hound Dog.* I was a kid, I liked dogs.

It was my mom who told me about the Beatles. They were on the radio in the car on our way to the Northshore shopping mall. She said, *Those are the Beatles.* I said, *Who?* I said it was stupid to have a name about insects.

The music! It was like being at the center of an explosion. Music was coming out of our pores, attacking from all directions, pushing and pulling and frying your brain. Suddenly you had anthems for everything in your life. The music owned your heart, your imagination, intellect, body. It all seemed perfectly timed. Has it always been like that? Or was it a special time?

That black-and-white yin-yang symbol, on a disk that spins? That's your teenage mind, spinning like a pinwheel, shooting sparks, spinning out of control. No wonder soldiers are 18, 19. You just want to charge blindly ahead, be a villain or a hero, be a force, kill or be killed.

The woman makes the decision. You have *no* say. Men are the expendable sex.

Fishing should be quiet, like meditation. It's the water, the fish, and you. You have to know the difference between a nibble and a bite. You can't set the hook on a nibble. You have to learn not to get excited. It's all patience, you put the fish out of your mind.

It's called fishing for a reason. If it were about catching, it'd be called catching. It's fishing. Instead of mindlessness like in Zen, it's fishlessness.

Football, poker, fishing. An old man's heaven. And a dog.

I call myself a cynical romantic. And an atheist Catholic. A social liberal and economic conservative. I don't bother trying to reconcile my conflicts. I'm an existentialist. I make decisions and take responsibility.

Sartre said we should live so we'll be missed. If I'm lucky, two people will miss me. What does that say about my life? It's like I just drifted through without making a shadow. Without a sound. A puff of smoke. Sartre also said Hell is other people. Guy was clued in.

Yea, I've got a great sense of humor. Because I'm bitter, bitter as hell. Don't get me started. That's why I laugh and joke. My three gods are Cynicism, Apathy, and Sarcasm. What's any of it matter?

Working backwards from the responses in several interviews, I have reconstructed what I think some of the questions might have been. Answer these questions—as always, picking and choosing among those offered or making up your own. Answers should be short—not more than a couple of sentences each. If you're not comfortable composing right on the computer, try this: Write your responses on 3x5 cards. Rearrange the cards to present your information in an order that seems best to you. Give the piece a title and type it up!

1. Background

   a. My father was _____. My mother was _____.

          nationality   same category

          religion

          profession

          temperament

   b. What were the consequences of that 'mix'?

    c. My dad/mom used to say _____.

    d. I was born and raised in _____.

    e. My mom and dad taught me a lot of things. I was raised to be _____.

    f. I'm so glad I _____.

2. Kids today have it much _____.

3. I never/always thought I would _____.

4. The hardest period of my life _____.

5. My definition of freedom:_____.

6. This is just a thought:_____.

    I'd like to weigh in on _____.

    You'll never find the answer to _____.

    I would argue that _____.

    It would be wrong to think that _____.

7. Someone said:_____.

8. There may come a day when _____.

9. Going forward, I _____.

FUN STUFF—ANECDOTES, ONE-LINERS, AND DIALOGUES

Here is an opportunity to showcase your wit—the stories and one-liners you tell over and over. Not jokes, but a manifestation of the wonderful, spontaneous humor of everyday life.

An **anecdote** is a short and amusing or interesting story about a real incident or person. Many times anecdotes reveal a truth or insight more general than the brief story itself. Sometimes an anecdote is just an anecdote.

> My longtime colleague, Al, asked me to take a late afternoon geometry class so he could keep an appointment. Since I taught mostly algebra, geometry was a novelty. I pranced back and forth in front of the class working the proofs, firing off extra questions, and offering up little tidbits about Euclid. The time went quickly.
>
> The bell rang and the kids filed out. A slender young man who had been sitting in the back of the room walked past me and said:
>
> "You're not a real sub, are you?"

Here's a family favorite.

BABEL

Mom, Bea, and I were chatting out in the kitchen. The conversation settled on "retention in children." Mom, a school psychologist, was talking about holding kids back a grade. Being a math teacher, I thought we were talking about memory issues. Bea, a biochemist, was thinking, urine?

🚐 HELPFUL HINT: ANECDOTE WRITING

A quick tip about writing up anecdotes. I start with a blank sheet of paper and write the punch line at the bottom. Then I go back up and figure out how to get there.

One-liners work well on a page of mixed formats or as fillers at the bottom of a page. You might try putting a border around them to separate them from the main focus of the page.

> Van Line: My friend Van is a pillar of the Gay community and a staunch Republican—a somewhat unusual combination.
>
> He says: "I'm so conservative, if I were straight I'd probably be anti-gay."

Dialogues put the reader at the scene and break up longer sections of prose.

One participant, writing for her daughters, shared this exchange with her mother who had Alzheimer's.

Alzheimer's is an awful disease. If one can laugh about some things, it makes it a little easier.

Mom: Why do you call me Mom?
Me: Because I'm your daughter.
Mom: You're not my daughter.
Me: Why don't you think I'm your daughter?
Mom: Because my daughter is much slimmer!

The next piece is by a participant who is a decorated urban middle-school volunteer tutor. This short piece speaks volumes about the heart of her involvement.

The seventh graders have to outline a story about Jackie Robinson. Delshay is working on a chapter about Robinson being court-martialed for taking the "wrong" seat on a bus on a military base.

DELSHAY: I don't get this stuff about the bus.
TUTOR: What stuff about the bus?
DELSHAY: When I get on a bus, I always go to the back. I like to ride in the back of the bus.
TUTOR: Choices, Delshay. It's about choices.

MICRO-MEMOIRS: SIX-WORD MEMOIRS, INVITATIONS, ADS, EMAILS, AND TEXTS

Six-Word Memoirs: The six-word memoir is just that—six words that capture a phase of your life. Good to know about. They are the epitome of the short piece. They sometimes show up in the *AARP* magazine. You can find a whole collection of them in *Six-Word Memoirs* edited by Smith Magazine.

My counselor thought I was dumb.
Hated school, hated work, love retirement.
Legal Notice: I've had it, Pal.
Death—what a way to go.

Invitations: Sometimes you can craft an idea in the form of an invitation, announcement, or classified ad. These alternatives allow you to lighten up an otherwise serious situation.

Mr. and Mrs. C. Howard Shaffer
invite you to celebrate the union
of their daughter, Susan
and
Ralph B.: 1965—1978
Thomas H.: 1979—1989
L. Jeffrey B.: 1990—1996
John S.: 2011—present

Texts and Emails make good incidental short pieces, too.

📖 PRINTING AND PRESERVING YOUR PLD

This is a good time to discuss the printing and binding of you PLD. The goal is to have multiple copies of your document to share with family and friends.

» Having your PLD printed and spiral bound turns out to be much simpler and cheaper than you might think. Most of the Elderwriters have gone to Staples or FedEx/Kinkos for the binding. (If you don't have Staples or FedEx/Kinko's in your locality, you probably have a local copy shop that provides these services.) You can have twenty to thirty pages spiral bound with a clear plastic cover on the front and a colored vinyl cover on the back for under $10.00. You can design your own title page, which will show through the clear cover. Very nice. They look terrific.

» For preservation purposes, you want your work to be printed on acid-free paper. Most office supply stores and copy shops sell acid-free paper that is ink jet and laser printer friendly. My choice was to print several copies of my document on my own printer. The title page was printed on decorative paper and added to the top of each copy. Then I took the completed PLDs to Staples to be bound.

» Copy shops offer other binding options, but the spiral binding holds up best. The employees at these copy facilities are very helpful. I believe you can take your disk or flash drive to them and they will print the pages for you. It may be something you want to check on.

» You may want to have photos restored or retouched before you have them scanned into your computer for use in your PLD. Look for these services in the Yellow Pages.

» There are specialty printing and graphic design businesses that will help you design and print your PLD. Cost will probably be several hundred dollars, but if money is no object, they do beautiful work. Again, check the Yellow Pages.

» Hobby and craft stores carry a variety of binders that allow you to include actual photos along with text. Most of their materials are of archival quality.

» Your local craft guilds may include someone with a specialty in book arts. These folks create beautiful hand made covers.

» Electronic Publishing—Someone in your family may be able to help you with these.

   1. Electronic books can be designed right on your Apple computer through iPhoto. Check with the nearest Apple store for information on this option.

   2. Online publishing of photo books that include text can be found at these websites:

>> www.blurb.com

>> www.lulu.com

>> www.shutterfly.com

>> www.createspace.com

>> www.unibook.com

I don't want you to feel overwhelmed. Visit your local copy shop. You will be delighted with your PLD.

☐ ☑ CHECKLIST—ANOTHER LOOK

At this point you probably have several completed pieces, a few works in progress, and a list of possible inclusions. Here is our checklist again. How are things going?

☐ Title Page

☐ Opening Letter

☐ Epigram/Epigraph

☐ List of Favorites

☐ Soothe Your Senses Poem

☐ Sayings, Quotations, Songs, Prayers by Others

☐ Pieces about Loved Ones Who Have Passed On

☐ Pieces about Loved Ones Still Here

☐ Pieces about Family History, Heirlooms, Treasures, Recipes

☐ Pieces about Your Family and Its Role in the Person You Are Today

☐ Pieces about What Matters to You, What's Important, What Gets You Fired Up

☐ Your Thoughts on Philosophical Themes—Love, Marriage, Friendship, Death, Religion, Justice

☐ The Impact of Historical Events on Your Life

☐ Personal Trials and Tribulations, Overcoming Adversity

☐ Some Fun Pieces Strategically Placed Throughout Your Document

☐ Any Photos or Family Documents You Wish to Include

☐ Closing Letter

✍ EXERCISE 26. ASSESSING YOUR PROGRESS

Peruse the list above and assess you work so far for balance—balance in your chosen topics, balance in your use of formats. Some Elderwriters have intentionally concentrated on one or two topics, one or two formats. That's fine, as long as it's intentional. If you want more variety, this is a time to adjust your game plan. Try working in an area where you have a gap.

CHAPTER 12

WINDING DOWN

IN CHAPTER 12 YOU WILL:

» be introduced to the Ethical Will

» consider apologies, regrets, eulogies, and obituaries

» consider a variety of ways to organize your PLD

» pick up a couple of hints

B Y CHAPTER 12 IT'S TIME to start winding down. Our celebration takes on a quieter tone. You need to begin thinking about the overall look of your PLD.

THE ETHICAL WILL

Earlier in this guide I mentioned the autobiography and memoir as two types of personal legacy writing. There is a third—the **ethical will**. There is nothing to prevent you from including an ethical will in your PLD or using the ethical will as a model for your opening and/or closing letter.

Ethical wills have been around since biblical times, but very few people know about them. The name is a little confusing. An ethical will is not a legal document.

An ethical will:

» is usually a one to three page end-of-life letter to loved ones.

» gives additional information, advice, or blessings to your heirs.

» provides an opportunity for an individual to share values, beliefs, life lessons, hopes for the future, love, and/or forgiveness with his/her family.

» is a written legacy document for the non-professional writer. It can be completed quite quickly.

It is my understanding that some legal and financial firms offer their clients assistance in composing an ethical will.

Here is a sample ethical will.

To My Dear Great-Grandchildren,

I am a very old man and you are very young. We live hundreds of miles apart. It is unlikely I will have a chance to speak to you about these things face to face.

I have lived through the most dynamic 97 years in human history. I have seen the best and the worst mankind has to offer. The best is better. Always choose tolerance and compassion over hate.

I was a physics teacher. I raised my children to trust the scientific method and eschew bluster, superstition, and emotion as a path to truth. I embraced the notion of a personal best—for myself and my children. If you're going to do something, do the best you can. Work at getting better. Improvement is key.

I had a good life partner—your great-grandmother. Fifty-five years of incompatibility. She was a real spark plug—bright, energetic, committed to her causes. She was always the liberal voice in the room. You're lucky to have her genes. That's important to me—that you have our genes—not just because that's our little slice of immortality, but because they're good genes. They will serve you well.

I'm not a formally religious man, but fifteen years ago I made a deal with the Lord that if I could just feed myself and take care of my own basic needs, I would never ask for anything again. We both kept our end of the bargain.

What do I wish for you? Productive satisfying lives, fun, optimism, resourcefulness. And I wish you good luck. So much of what happens to us is luck. I wish you the good kind.

With love,
Your Great-Grandad

Dr. Barry Baines's book, *Ethical Wills,* is an excellent resource for those wishing to create an ethical will. In addition to his informative guidebook, Dr. Baines maintains a website with some fifty examples of ethical wills. (www.ethicalwill.com)

Jo Kline Cebuhar, JD in her recent book, *So Grows the Tree: Creating an Ethical Will* takes the reader beyond the traditional ethical will and ventures into other memorabilia. It is an excellent resource for the PLD enthusiast.

✍ EXERCISE 27. YOUR OPENING LETTER REVISITED

Take a look at some of the sample ethical wills at www.ethicalwill.com. Have you been able to complete your opening letter? This would be a good time to polish that up.

▣ APOLOGIES, REGRETS, EULOGIES, AND OBITUARIES

1.   Rarely have Elderwriters brought **apology** or **regret** pieces to class. Have they written them? Very possibly, but they have not been seen as something to share.

Apologies and regrets have different levels of intensity. The PLD is not a confessional. On the other hand, there may be situations you would like to acknowledge. Things like:

> » Paths not taken/words not spoken
> » Times when you were not generous, caring, attentive, or patient enough
> » Flaws of character
> » Unintended consequences
> » Giving up too soon
> » Not standing up for what you believe

Apologies and regrets can be tucked into letters or poems, mentioned in a short memoir, or just listed. Here is a good, low intensity list by one of the Elderwriters.

THINGS I WISH I HAD DONE

Gotten a motorized wheelchair for my Dad when he was in the nursing home.

Hugged Angie on her last day at Kodak instead of looking forward to having her company for a few weeks and anticipating her next position.

Bought Xerox at $7 a share.

Retired sooner, before I got sick.

Learned Spanish or French or Italian.

Painted more.

Played the piano more.

Learned to play the guitar before my fingers got stiff.

2.   Many PLDs contain **eulogies** participants gave, or wish they had. We lose loved ones without the opportunity to say a few words. Here's your chance.

This is Barb Anderson's eulogy to her much loved stepmother, Martha.

What a privilege to have been loved and cared for by Martha. There was never a time when she didn't consider me "hers." For 61 years she was, and will continue to be, my MENTOR, MY MOTHER, MY FRIEND.

It was a tremendous project to take on an 11-year-old when she was only 23. But she gave us a wonderful family—including the sisters I always wanted. And one thing I must say is that I feel she gave my father the only real happiness he had ever known.

The courage she showed when she went on to school and raised the girls is an example for all.

She loved my husband as a son and she and Duane were with us every single step of the way through his journey. The comfort they gave us made so much possible.

There are many things to share but the most important is my love for Martha and hers for all of us. There is a message on the wall at Sara's house that I always read and think of Martha.

Some people come into our lives and quickly go.

Some people move our souls to dance

They awaken us to a new understanding with the passing whisper of their wisdom.

Some people make the sky more beautiful to gaze upon.

They stay in our lives awhile, leave footprints on our hearts and we are never the same.

With great love I say there are the same number of letters in Martha and Mother, and I never knew the difference.

3. One of our participants wrote an ingenious piece from the perspective of herself as the deceased listening to someone giving *her* eulogy. It started with:

She was a good woman, a good mother, a good friend.
Gee, I wish they had said those things about me while I was alive.

4. You may want to create and include a piece to be read at your own funeral—possibly using an ethical will format. Why leave it up to someone who doesn't know you so well?

5. **Obituaries** also find their way into PLDs. One of our participants and her husband sat down and wrote dual obituaries as part of her PLD project. There was some discussion of whether or not to use the term *loving* spouse.

6. Copies of obituaries may be part of the family memorabilia you include in your document. By design, they give a lot of information in a short space.

✍ EXERCISE 28. CONSIDER COMPOSING YOUR EULOGY

Consider composing a letter or eulogy to be shared at your funeral or memorial service. Include it in your PLD.

📖 ORGANIZING YOUR DOCUMENT

Now that you have several completed pieces, it's time to plan the overall organization of your document. Let's look at some strategies.

> » Write the names of your pieces on 3x5 cards. Spread them out on the dining room table. Experiment with grouping them together under some concept. Is there some natural organization of your work?
> » Chronological order—certainly the most obvious. Start with family history pieces, childhood, adolescence, young adult—and so on. Very serviceable.
> » Organize by the seasons of your life—Spring, Summer, Autumn, Winter.
> » Use a flashback approach—start with a couple of pieces about your life now, then transition back to the early days. End with today and looking forward.
> » Some of our Elderwriters have written specialty documents—the Women in My Life, Family Christmas. These are easy to organize.
> » You can start with a table of contents and just line up the pieces.
> » One of our participants created a personal inventory table of contents:

I am
Woman
Daughter
Sibling
Teacher
Sister in Christ
Caretaker
Retiree

The placement of her pieces corresponded to the inventory. What a gem!

» In my own document—which, of course, was written before I came in contact with the Elderwriters and their wonderful, creative ideas—the main topics are randomly placed. That works, too.

HELPFUL HINT: ON BORROWING, ADAPTING, ADOPTING

One of our participants recently mentioned that she pays much more attention to how books are set up since she started writing her PLD.

The Book Thief by Markus Zusak, in addition to being a wonderful read, is an example I often use. It has some organizing strategies that could easily be borrowed, adapted, adopted for use in your PLD.

Each part of the book (there are ten parts) starts off with a title and listing of the names of the chapters. Sounds like the usual, but it looks different. In your document, this technique might result in:

Part One
FAMILY HISTORY
featuring
Grampa Comes to America—Uncle Bob Changes His Name—The New Shoes
Losing the Farm—Celeste—Right from Wrong

Part Two
MY CHILDHOOD
Featuring
First Day of School...and so on.

As you read books, magazines, and newspapers take notice of these presentation ideas that might work well in your PLD. They give you additional options for customizing your document.

Chapter 13

Wrapping Up

In Chapter 13 you will:

» plan a closing letter or statement

» be introduced to the ideas of writing for others, youngerwriters, and becoming an Elderwriters facilitator

» receive a fond farewell from this facilitator

Closing Letter or Statement

How do you wrap up your PLD? A **closing letter or statement** gives you an opportunity to reaffirm what you have written, share your intentions for the future, and offer final blessings and well wishes to your family.

Here's my closing letter to my boys:

Dear V and Z —

 I began to get suspicious when the Helping Hands guys in the supermarket parking lot started asking me if I needed assistance. *Assistance, indeed. Who are these chumps?* Slowly my self-image is adjusting to reality.

 Here's my calculus for old age: As long as I can muster kindness and compassion for others, I have a positive presence. When my world gets so small I can think only of myself, it's time to turn out the lights. Not always a choice. We shall see.

For now, I have my new family of four, places to go, things to do. I'm a lucky woman. I still buy green bananas.

You are the proverbial wind beneath my wings. Take care of each other.

I love you,
Mom

Some Elderwriters have chosen to compose a "My Life Going Forward" piece outlining their plans for the future.

✍ EXERCISE 29. PUT AN END TO THE PROJECT

Here's the final exercise. Keep writing until you've said what you want to say, then put an end to the project. Don't let it drag on. Pack up your work and head off to the copy shop. You'll be glad you did.

FINAL COMMENTS: WRITING FOR OTHERS; ELDERWRITERS/ YOUNGERWRITERS; BECOMING A FACILITATOR

There are a couple of issues I would like to comment on before I go.

- » Writing for Others—There may be people in your family or circle of friends who would like to prepare a personal legacy document but are unable to do so on their own—individuals who are developmentally or otherwise disabled, very elderly, or dying. Writing for others is a topic unto itself but may be something for you to think about.

- » Elderwriters/Youngerwriters—Elderwriters are my cohort. I have pitched this book at folks like myself. Logically, of course, legacy writing can be done at any time in your life. The same emphasis on short pieces and varied landscape is valuable whenever you decide to put pen to paper.

- » Interested in facilitating an Elderwriters class yourself? I have included some Tips for Facilitators in Appendix D.

My Sendoff

What has kept me going through this personal legacy writing endeavor is the tremendous pride and sense of accomplishment the Elderwriters have shown and the camaraderie and support they have given each other. It has been an honor to be part of their success.

Lastly, let me say I know personal legacy writing is neither a simple nor an easy task. It takes concentration, perseverance, and a certain amount of courage. I salute you!

Good luck in all you do.

Sue Barocas
2013

Appendix A:
Introduction to Writing Groups

Some people feel they work best alone. Others are inspired by the camaraderie and support of a group.

Group time has been an important component of the success of the Elderwriters classes. Some participants would say it is the most important component. For that reason I am including information about writing groups here in Appendix A.

Remember, two is a group. If you don't have the makings of a group in your immediate area, perhaps you have a friend or family member with whom you can correspond. **A word of caution:** Don't share personal information with a stranger in an unsupervised situation.

Writing groups generally have four to six members. Each class we spend thirty to forty minutes on group time.

I. Why Work in a Group?
- » To try out your pieces on others and see if you're having the effect you want
- » To get ideas from other people
- » To build confidence in yourself and other group members
- » To encourage each other to keep writing
- » To provide good examples for each other
- » To get help/suggestions from each other
- » To reduce isolation

II. When giving feedback:

Do:

» Accentuate the positive

» Use your own perspective

» Keep your comments brief

» Stay focused

» Listen carefully

» Maintain confidentiality

Don't:

» Instruct or nitpick

» Be negative

» Interrupt the reader

» Get into arguments over positions other than your own

» Draw comparisons

» Dominate the discussion

III. What are you giving/getting feedback on?

» Clarity

» Did the piece achieve its purpose?

» Wording

» Format

» Tone

» Other problems

IV. Sample comments (keep them positive, constructive, and helpful):

» I loved the poem at the end of the paragraph. I'm going to try that.

» I would like to see you elaborate on __.

» The Latin phrase was the perfect ending because...

» Your use of the present tense was interesting because...

» The punch line was great. Personally, I would have gotten there a little sooner.

» You must have loved her very much.

It is each participant's responsibility to bring something to read. Pieces should be limited to one page. If your piece is longer, select part of it to share. If possible, bring copies for members of your group to look at while you read.

The copies should be returned to you when the discussion of your piece is over. Group members may ask to keep the copy of your piece as a model of something they would like to try. Sometimes you don't mind; sometimes you do. To avoid any awkwardness, let the group know up front you will be collecting the copies if that is your choice.

Each individual reads his/her piece and the group comments. Simple as that. If people do not have a new, original piece to read, they may bring something they have written in the past or a selection by another author that they intend to put in their document. Occasionally individuals canvass the rest of the group for ideas regarding a work in progress.

Whatever you bring to share is an important contribution to the group.

Appendix B:
Personal Legacy Writing
Reading List

Writing/Memoir Writing

Croft, Mary K., and Joyce S. Steward. *The Leisure Pen: A Book for Elderwriters.* Palmer Publications, Inc., 1988.

Fershleisher, Rachel, and Larry Smith, eds. *Not Quite What I Was Planning: Six-Word Memoirs by Writers Famous and Obscure, from* Smith Magazine. New York: Harper Perennial,2008.

Gutkind, Lee. *The Art of Creative Nonfiction: Writing and Selling the Literature of Reality.* New York: John Wiley and Sons, Inc., 1997.

Miller, Brenda, and Suzanne Paola. *Tell It Slant: Writing and Shaping Creative Nonfiction.* New York: McGraw-Hill, 2005.

Spence, Linda. *Legacy: A Step-by-Step Guide to Writing Personal History.* Athens, OH: Swallow Press, 1997.

Stanek, Lou Willett. *Writing Your Life: Putting Your Past on Paper.* New York: HarperCollins Publishers, 1996.

Tiberghien, Susan M. *One Year to a Writing Life: Twelve Lessons to Deepen Every Writer's Art and Craft.* Cambridge, MA: Da Capo Press, 2007.

Oral History

Hart, Cynthia, and Lisa Samson. *The Oral History Workshop: Collect and Celebrate the Life Stories of Your Family and Friends.* New York: Workman Publishing, 2009.

Poetry

Mehta, Diane. *How to Write Poetry: The Ultimate Guide to Putting It All Together, In Your Head and On The Page.* Spark Publishing, 2008.

Raffel, Burton. *How to Read a Poem.* New York: Penguin Group, 1984.

Woolridge, Susan Goldsmith. *Poemcrazy: Freeing Your Life with Words.* New York: Three Rivers Press, 1996.

Writing Groups

Cole, Joni B. *Toxic Feedback: Helping Writers Survive and Thrive.* Lebanon, NH: University Press of New England, 2006.

LeGuin, Ursula K. *Steering the Craft: Exercises and Discussions on Story Writing for the Lone Navigator or the Mutinous Crew.* Portland, OR: The Eighth Mountain Press, 1998.

Ethical Wills

Baines, Barry K. *Ethical Wills: Putting Your Values on Paper, Second Edition.* Cambridge, MA: Da Capo Press, 2006.

Cebuhar, Jo Kline. *So Grows the Tree: Creating an Ethical Will: The Legacy of Your Beliefs and Values, Life Lessons and Hopes for the Future.* West Des Moines, IA: Murphy Publishing, 2010.

Journal Writing

Adams, Kathleen. *Journal to the Self: Twenty-Two Paths to Personal Growth: Open the Door to Self-Understanding by Writing, Reading, and Creating a Journal of Your Life.* New York: Grand Central Publishing, 1990.

Rico, Gabriele. *Writing the Natural Way.* New York: Tarcher, 2000.

SHORT CREATIVE NONFICTION

Jones, Mary Paumier, and Judith Kitchen, eds. *In Short: A Collection of Brief Creative Nonfiction.* New York: W.W. Norton and Company, 1996.

Livingston, Sonja. *Ghostbread.* Athens, GA: University of Georgia Press, 2009.

Sutin, Lawrence. *A Postcard Memoir.* Saint Paul, MN: Graywolf Press, 2000

Appendix C:
Summary of Writing Exercises

Exercise 1. A Few of Your Favorite Things—page 8

Let's try something. Here's a good place to start: the grossly underrated LIST. Probably the most accessible literary form there is. Make a list of twenty to twenty-five of your favorite things, just one or two words each. It's as simple as that.

I love these lists. They say so much about you with a minimum of time and effort. There are always a few surprises in them. It's a great piece to put in your PLD.

Exercise 2. The Senses—page 9

Now that you've made a list of your favorite things, write a poem or set of sentences that catalogs those things that soothe your senses, your soul. These are important elements of your personality. Share them.

The sight of _____

The sound of _____

The feel of _____

The taste of _____

The smell of _____

The thought of _____

Lots of opportunities here for putting your own personal twist on the shape and composition of the piece.

✍ EXERCISE 3. YOUR COLLECTION OF SAYINGS—PAGE 12

Put together a little collection of your favorite sayings that you can draw on as your legacy writing moves forward. These one-liners will provide inspiration, clarification, and enhancement to your work.

Examples:

> » Albert Finney on being asked how he felt about turning 70: "I don't think about my age. I think about my time—and my time is now."
> » Life's messy.
> » The only behavior you really can change is your own.
> » Be brave.

✍ EXERCISE 4. USING THE MEMORY RETRIEVAL EXERCISE—PAGE 14

Use the memory retrieval exercise to help you resurrect the details of a special event in your life. At this point, just worry about gathering the data. Later, your written account may take any form—a paragraph, vignette, narrative, poem, letter…you'll find your comfort zone.

✍ EXERCISE 5. A CLUSTERING ACTIVITY—PAGE 16

Try doing the clustering/mind-mapping exercise on a topic of your choice—a friend, sibling, other relative, holiday tradition, a concept from the basic themes list—then organize your data to create a piece. Put your own personal spin on it.

✍ EXERCISE 6. WRITING ABOUT SOMEONE YOU LOVE AND ADMIRE—PAGE 20

One of the primary goals of personal legacy writing is to share with friends, family, and future generations what life has meant to you—who you are, what's important, what matters. What you say about the people you love and admire says a lot about you. Short vignettes can open a window onto your life while paying tribute to loved ones.

Reread Helgi Mepham's piece about her father and Gwen Tucker's piece about her great-grandfather. Think of a friend, relative, mentor, famous person, or pet you would like to honor with a piece in your legacy document. Give it a go.

✍ Exercise 7. Keeping a List of *ah, aha,* and *haha* Moments—page 22

The *ah, aha,* and *haha* are everyday moments that stand out in your mind—the extraordinary in the ordinary. For now, just keep a running list of these moments. Wait to write them up until you have a few more formats under your belt.

✍ Exercise 8. The Wild Card ☺—page 24

The Wild Card allows you to ignore the constraints of my suggestions and create your own exercise. Go for it! Please join me again in Chapter 4.

✍ Exercise 9. Setting Up a Guidelines for Living File—page 30

Set up a Guidelines for Living file. This page will be a work-in-progress for some time. Revisit your collection of sayings and quotations. Write down the one-liners you use over and over. Consider the beliefs you hold that motivate your actions and influence the way you treat others. Return to this page regularly until you are satisfied that it accurately represents your personal outlook. Then type it up and put it in the completed pile.

✍ Exercise 10. Writing Up a Preliminary Table of Contents—page 33

Write up a preliminary table of contents for your document. Consider involving other members of your family—children, spouse, siblings—in your legacy writing endeavor. Ask them what they would like to see included in your document.

✍ Exercise 11. Writing a Very Short Memoir Piece—page 41

Aim to have at least two or three short memoir pieces in your document. Their impact is in their brevity. If your writing takes more than half a page, whittle it down. Use the Memory Retrieval Exercise to recreate the details. Short memoirs are a wonderful way to *Celebrate Your Life!*

✍ Exercise 12. A Time Capsule—page 41

For a little change of pace—try a Time Capsule. Suppose you have a metal box 1ft x 1 ft x 1.5 ft.. As of today, what eight or ten items would you put in the box if you knew it wasn't going to be opened for one hundred years? What indispensable twenty first century paraphernalia would you drop in there? Keep it light-hearted.

✍ Exercise 13. Write a Poem Using the Kobylak Form—page 52

Wesley Kobylak has used a flexible format—a combination of prose and poetry lines—in a piece from his chapbook, *Moments*.

The pattern is: One long sentence, three short phrases. One long sentence, three short phrases.

Very effective. Easy to work with. I used this form for poems in my own document.

Write a poem utilizing the 'Kobylak' form. You may want to start with clustering to gather data for your piece. The long sentences are key. They set the stage for the short phrases. You'll be surprised at how well this works.

✍ Exercise 14. Try an Acrostic—page 53

Liz Rowsick is the source of several very creative legacy pieces. Read through her acrostic about a treasured visit to her son in Ch. 6

Each line is *not* a complete sentence. The sentences wrap around to the next line. This gives the piece a different feel.

Try your hand at an acrostic. See what you come up with.

✍ Exercise 15. Writing a Letter for Your PLD—page 57

Reread the bullets about letters. Find one that appeals to you and craft a letter. If you don't have any ideas right now, put this on your to-do list and come back to it.

✍ Exercise 16. Begin Work on an Opening Letter—page 59

Begin work on an opening letter, even if it's just to set up a folder.

✍ EXERCISE 17. CREATING A VIRTUAL MEMORY BOX—PAGE 65

Create a Virtual Memory Box for someone and include it in your PLD.

✍ EXERCISE 18. BUILD-A-PAGE—PAGE 69

Try creating a specialty page of your own.

Look over the Basic Themes and Special Topics list. Highlight a topic you think might be the focus of a page in your PLD. Set up a manila folder for the page.

- » Brainstorm the topic using the clustering technique.
- » Gather up any sayings or quotes by others you might want to use.
- » As we cover additional formats, revisit your topic and experiment with new ways to collect your thoughts and share your feelings.

Try using different fonts to highlight the various components of your page.

✍ EXERCISE 19. WRITING A FAMILY HISTORY PIECE—PAGE 72

The family history piece is an excellent inclusion in your PLD. If you have the information, give it a go!

✍ EXERCISE 20. WRITING A PERSONAL LEGACY ESSAY—PAGE 75

The personal legacy essay provides an important link between you and your childhood—a link your descendents will not understand or appreciate unless you tell them. Make this essay a priority. You will be glad you did.

Consider some demographic that impacted your family or set it apart from others in your community—ethnicity, religious affiliation, economic status, number of siblings, language, profession, illness, height/weight, quirks. How did that situation affect your childhood and contribute to your personality/philosophy today? Start crafting a personal legacy essay to include in your PLD.

✍ EXERCISE 21. TRYING YOUR HAND AT A STUFF PIECE—PAGE 79

Try your hand at composing a stuff piece. Your stuff piece might be in the form of a poem or letter. Recall Pam Erwin's poem about her piano in Chapter 6. Start with the object and see where it takes you. Good luck!

✐ EXERCISE 22. WRITING A PERSONAL ESSAY—PAGE 85

Every PLD should contain at least one personal essay type piece. Find your topic, then find your voice. Revisit the Basic Themes and Special Topics chart in Chapter 1 for ideas.

✐ EXERCISE 23. WRITING ABOUT AN AREA IN WHICH YOU EXCEL—PAGE 85

Identify an area in which you excel. Is this a natural talent or something you have cultivated through study and hard work? Discuss how this expertise makes you feel. How has it added to the overall quality of your life?

✐ EXERCISE 24. WRITING ABOUT A LIFE-CHANGING EXPERIENCE—PAGE 91

Have you, or someone in your family, had to deal with a life-changing experience? Write a piece—or a collage of pieces—that share the facts, reactions, and reflections on the situation.

✐ EXERCISE 25. PEOPLE WON'T KNOW THE REAL YOU UNLESS YOU TELL THEM—PAGE 94

Interviews are usually in Q and A form. *Esquire* magazine does an interesting thing with their interviews of famous people. You never see the questions. What appears in the magazine (and online at www.esquire.com/features/what-ive-learned) are the one to five sentence answers, separated by a couple of blank lines, presented as a personal statement. The entire interview is one or two pages long. The theme is always some variation on "what I've learned."

Try your hand at an interview piece.

✐ EXERCISE 26. ASSESSING YOUR PROGRESS—PAGE 101

Peruse the checklist and assess you work so far for balance—balance in your chosen topics, balance in your use of formats. Some Elderwriters have intentionally concentrated on one or two topics, one or two formats. That's fine, as long as it's intentional. If you want more variety, this is a time to adjust your game plan. Try working in an area where you have a gap.

✍ **EXERCISE 27. YOUR OPENING LETTER REVISITED—PAGE 105**

Take a look at some of the sample ethical wills at www.ethicalwill.com. Have you been able to complete your opening letter? This would be a good time to polish that up.

✍ **EXERCISE 28. CONSIDER COMPOSING YOUR EULOGY—PAGE 107**

Consider composing a letter or eulogy to be shared at your funeral or memorial service. Include it in your PLD.

✍ **EXERCISE 29. PUT AN END TO THE PROJECT—PAGE 110**

Here's the final exercise. Keep writing until you've said what you want to say, then put an end to the project. Don't let it drag on. Pack up your work and head off to the copy shop. You'll be glad you did.

Appendix D:
Tips for Facilitators

» **Interested in facilitating an Elderwriters class?**

This guide makes it easy. Retirees, teachers, librarians, social workers, and medical professionals are likely facilitator candidates. There are many more. Warmth and enthusiasm are a must. I recommend class sizes of six to twelve.

» **Who would sponsor an Elderwriters Personal Legacy Writing Course?**

The Elderwriters course is appropriate for any organizations, agencies, or other groups committed to lifelong learning, continuing education, or quality of life for seniors.

To name a few:

AAUW	Public Libraries
Book Clubs	Retirement Organizations
Bookstores	Senior Citizen Centers
Churches and Synagogues	Senior Citizen Complexes
Continuing Education Programs	Veteran's Outreach
Council for the Aging	YMCA
Gilda's Club	

» The original Elderwriters course is designed to meet an hour and a half a week for six to eight weeks. If participants have not completed their PLDs in that time—and many do not—they can organize small groups on their own to continue meeting after the formal class is over.

» We always begin with a little *How's it going?* session. We do not write in class—writing is done at home. Class time is divided between discussing the material in the chapters and writing groups.

» You will need some facilitating supplies—nametags, some large paper/white board to write on, markers, a box of tissues. Check out the room you will be using before the first class. You will need seating that allows you to break the class into writing groups of four to six.

» Your role as a facilitator will be greatly enhanced if you have created a PLD for yourself. That's the best training.

» Do a little reconnaissance work to locate copy shops and binding facilities in your area. Participants will want to know where to purchase acid-free paper.

» Many people are sensitive about their writing. They think it isn't good enough, they aren't skilled enough, no one will be interested. They are self-conscious in front of others. They need encouragement and understanding. There are no failures, no letters of rejection in an Elderwriters class.

APPENDIX E:
SAMPLE PERSONAL LEGACY DOCUMENT

Snapshots of My Life

Susan Shaffer Barocas
1943—

2011

Dear Victor and Zachary,

At 67, I knew I didn't have enough to do when I started thinking about getting a tattoo.

I'm not old enough to just sit and wait, I said to a friend.

You're never old enough for that, she replied.

I decided to reactivate my long- standing interest in creative writing, with the idea of compiling a document I could leave you boys. Well, here it is. This scrapbook of writings reflects my thoughts and feelings about what life has meant to me. It was a rewarding and enlightening project.

At my age, every day is a gift—but the greatest gift of all, is you.

Love,
Mom

"You have to fight for your life. That's the chief condition under which you hold it. Then why be halfhearted?"

Saul Bellow, *Herzog*

GUIDELINES AND INSIGHTS

Every now and then, I hear a statement, or have an insight, that I find myself returning to again and again. These guidelines have become an integral part of my personal decision-making apparatus.

1. The only behavior you can change is your own.
2. If you don't want to do something, one reason is as good as another.
3. If you don't like your life, change it.
4. Find something that will bring joy to your life.
5. You can accomplish as much as you want as long as you don't care who gets the credit.
6. You learn more by listening than by talking.
7. People do the best they can under the circumstances.
8. A sense of entitlement is the root of much evil.
9. Mediocrity is not a behavioral constraint.
10. The John Henry Conjecture: Don't fight technology—technology will win.
11. Expect variation.
12. Look backward 20% and forward 80%.

A Few of My Favorite Things

» America—democracy, rule of law, diversity, hope

» large animals

» changing seasons

» cooking

» day trips

» dogs/Emma

» eating

» enough money

» first and last hour of the day

» my sons/family

» friends

» good health

» Inuit prints

» the Law of Cosines

» learning new things

» Abraham Lincoln

» the marimba

» movies

» live musical and dramatic performances

» nature

» the Normal Curve

» New York State

» polynomial functions

» reading/thinking

» my house

» thunderstorms/blizzards/wind

» retirement

» words

Things that Inspire Awe

- » genius
- » the human body
- » mathematics
- » natural disasters
- » panoramic views
- » reproduction
- » science and technology

Favorite Books

Fiction:

Herzog by Saul Bellow
Aloft by Chang-rae Lee
Samuel Johnson is Indignant by Lydia Davis

Nonfiction:

The Nine by Jeffrey Toobin
Team of Rivals by Doris Kearns Goodwin
Too Big to Fail by Andrew Ross Sorkin
Lincoln on Race and Slavery edited by Henry Louis Gates Jr. and Donald Yacavone

Biographies:

Genius by James Gleick
American Prometheus by Kai Bird and Martin J. Sherwin
Gertrude Bell by Georgina Howell

Memoir:

Survival in Auschwitz by Primo Levi

Children:

Who Took the Farmer's Hat? By Joan L. Nodset
The Wonderful Wings of Harold Harrabescu by Georgess McHargue
The Blind Men and the Elephant retold by Lillian Quigley
Owen and Mzee (nonfiction) by Isabella and Craig Hatkoff and Paula Kahumbu

FAVORITE MOVIES

» *Rocky* (1976)

» *Midnight Run* (1988)

» *The Adventures of Priscilla, Queen of the Desert* (1994)

» *Billy Eliot* (2000)

» *Frozen River* (2008)

» *Mao's Last Dancer* (2009)

My Team

My team is getting smaller. Important players have died. The rules have changed. The goals are different.

These Men

Who are these men?
My babies, my boys,
these men.

Grown-ups with wives
    and separate lives.
Dreams unfurled,
    you throw back your shoulders
    and meet the world.

Far away, going gray,
    you'll always stay—
my babies, my boys,
these men.

✿

My Grandchildren

Grand children
Son flowers
Someday I may
    Know them well.

✿

My Sister

I have known my sister all my life and still she amazes me
    with her depth
    her logic
    her humor.
She will leave her world a better place than she found it.
    She is a
    Good Woman.
    Bea.

☼

SCWT
(Soft-Coated Wheaten Terrier)

I'm drinking coffee
    in the big chair.
She stares at me—I put down my cup.
    I am well trained.
With both hands
    I tap the top of my chest twice
    and hold out my arms.
A moment of flight;
    a four-point landing in my lap.
She licks my ear
    and perches on the arm of the chair
    like a leprechaun.
Soft-coated love.
Emma.

☼

A late entry on the team—
Great promise
JHS
Que sera, sera

When I was a child, we lived in the farmhouse of a small retirement farm owned and operated by my grandfather.

The Shaffer Compound

^^Pasture^^   ^^Pasture^^   ^^Pasture^^

THE BARN   ^^^Garden^^^

5976 Broadway   **5986 Broadway**   **5990 Broadway**
The Farmhouse   **My Grandparents plus**   **Uncle Fritz and**
Mom, Dad, Barb   **Great Aunt Deed and**   **Aunt Virginia**
and Me   **Uncle Jimmy**

This was my known world.

Uncle Jimmy (1903-1987) was an artist—mostly oils: portraits and flowers. He was good enough to be part of a circle of Western New York artists; not good enough to be in museums other than the local historical society. Although my grandparents' home contained many of Jimmy's oil paintings, someone must have been particularly fond of the Indian.

My best guess is that Jimmy drew the Indian in the 1920s when he was in art school. It is a wonderful charcoal rendering of the side of an Indian's face. The piece measures 16 x 25 inches. It was prominently displayed in the parlor behind my grandfather's rocking chair. The two of them—Grandad and the Indian—watched over the farm and family and greeted me on my daily visits. It never occurred to me to ask who he was or what he was doing there.

When Jimmy died, I had the Indian carefully reframed. He now hangs to the left of my fireplace. I can't miss him. He does not blend well with the Inuit prints that fill my walls. It doesn't matter. At one point, I tried moving him to a less conspicuous spot. I couldn't do it. I could NOT do it. He is the guardian of my childhood, the sentinel of my heritage. It is still his watch.

He is the Indian in the living room.

AMERICA

America, YOU are my country.
      Bride of Democracy, daughter of the Rule of Law
      Home of the tired and the poor.
      Of the people, by the people, for the people
      That's you, America
YOU are my country.

America, you ARE my country.
      You did some bad things.
      Slavery? Discrimination?
      Reservation? Occupation?
      You're a work in progress, America
But, you ARE my country.

America, you are MY country.
      You make me want to be a better citizen.
      Right the wrongs, give back, lend-a-hand
      You make my heart beat faster, America
You are MY country.

America, you are my COUNTRY.
      Even the Golden Arches and smokestacks
      and traffic jams can't diminish your beauty.
      …from sea to shining sea. Sing it, Ray!
America, you are my COUNTRY.

…and I love you.

☞ **9 Things To Do if Your Life Starts to Unravel**

1. Stick to a schedule.
2. Exercise/lose weight.
3. Stay well groomed.
4 .Clean your nest.
5. Keep current with your insurance.
6. Join a support group/get professional help.
7. Reinvent yourself.
8. Read *The Economist.*
9. Keep firing.

On Marriage/Relationships

Mr. and Mrs. C. Howard Shaffer
invite you to celebrate the union
of their daughter, Susan,
and
Ralph B. : 1965—1978
Thomas H. : 1979—1989
Jeffrey B. : 1990—1996
John S. : 2011—present

When Jeff and I went down to City Hall to get a marriage license, the sign over the counter read:

> Dog Licenses
> Fishing Licenses
> Marriage Licenses

It should have been a head's up.

Are these the words of Artie Shaw? They could be mine. "My divorces have been much more successful than my marriages. I never had a divorce that didn't last."

Never Give Up—Spring 2012

AARP has some TV ads that feature 60 year-olds saying what they want to be when they grow up. One of the women says, "I want to fall in love again."

Well, hey, I did! There he was at our 50th high school reunion—funny, caring, available, with cat—my new life partner(s).

And he thinks he snagged the prom queen. What a hoot!

God, Religion, Spirituality

A Jew by choice, I have never been totally confident of my place in the Jewish community. Relatively few people were converting to Judaism in the 1960s. I have a particularly fond memory of the attendant in the mikvah. She wore the chilling numerals from Auschwitz on the inside of her wrist. She welcomed me. "So many are leaving the faith," she said, "it's good to see you are coming in." Rabbi Abraham Karp, a prominent social activist, performed the ceremony.

Many years later, after I retired, I was part of an adult B'nai Mitzvot class at Temple Sinai. Reading from the Torah was an unexpectedly moving and rewarding experience, as was seeing Victor sitting proudly in the front row.

✡

Prayer has not played a large part in my life. I do not know a personal God. I did, however, come across a reference to prayer in our new reform siddur that struck a chord. (January 2011)

Pray as if everything depended on God.
Act as if everything depended on you.

I have never really understood spirituality.

Digression: **Guess Who?**

Who is the most famous Jewish mother of all time?
Dody Goodman?
Nope.
Totie Fields?
Nope.
Golda Meir?
Nope.
I give up.
The Virgin Mary.

Death, Burial, and the Hereafter

1996

One Friday night in late October, I met Gram and Grandad at Ripa's to celebrate my birthday. The conversation meandered around until Gram announced, "I've joined TAP." Somewhat incredulous, I asked, "You're dancing?"

Her face lit up and she laughed like a schoolgirl. "No, no," she sputtered. "It's the Telephone Assistance Program."

I realized I hadn't seen her laugh like that in a very long time.

I never saw her again. She died in her sleep on Thanksgiving night. We had planned to meet for brunch at Bob Evan's in Batavia on Friday. She stood me up.

2009

"Away Back Home in Indiana"—the last song I sang with my dad. Neither of us ever lived in Indiana.

My ashes will be buried in the Rural Cemetery, Lot 12, Section 3W, Grave 5—right next to my folks, who are in grave 4. They're waiting for me.

The Hereafter

My fantasy of the Hereafter looks like a scene from a Samuel Beckett play. The stage is dark and foggy. A single streetlamp dimly illuminates one of those slatted green benches you see at a bus stop. At the left end of the bench, close to the light, my mom sits holding a newborn tightly wrapped in a light blanket, as newborns often are. Next to her is my dad, wearing grey sweatpants, a navy blue sweater, and bowling shoes. His arm is draped casually along the back of the bench, behind Mom. They seem to be chatting.

Martha sits next to Daddy, her legs primly crossed at the knee. She is reading a book. A black and white Australian Shepherd lies at her feet. The rest of the bench is empty.

Marcia B. Shaffer—April 10, 1919—Thanksgiving, 1996
C. Howard Shaffer—July 24, 1912—September 16, 2009
Noah Barocas—March 5, 1968—March 6, 1968
Martha Kelly—July 26, 1934—February 19, 2005
Roxanne—died June 22, 2010

They live in my heart.

THE RITUAL—FOR NOAH, WHO LIVED ONLY A FEW HOURS

On March 5th I take the blue tapestry pouch from the closet in the hall.
    The birth certificate is there.
    March 5, 1968
    Baby boy—our Noah.

In my mind, I kiss his little hands and feet.
    I press his cheek to mine.
    He feels my tears.
    I tell him I love him.

On March 6th, I replace the pouch.
    Until next year,
    A mother mourning
    Forever.

I wholeheartedly bought into LBJ's War on Poverty. Education was the answer. Urban teaching was the path to take. From 1975—2001, I approached the teaching of high school mathematics at Wilson Magnet High School with something akin to missionary zeal.

I did not make a difference. If anything, the African American academic situation was worse when I retired than when I began, because hope was dwindling. African American underachievement remains an insoluble problem. It is arguably this nation's most tragic failure.

Success Story: (early 1990s)

Early September...opening day of school...new students, old teacher. I have 180 days to impress on these kids the meaning and importance of mathematics.

Malik and Maurice sit side by side near the front—two gangly, flightless birds perched behind their desks—black faces, white teeth, 9th grade optimism.

Malik glances from me to the framed *Time* magazine cover hanging at the side of the blackboard—Geena Davis and Susan Sarandon.

"I know why you put that picture there," he says, pointing. "You look like one of those women."

"Yeah?" I ask. "Which one?"

"The one on the right."

"No," counters Maurice, "the one on the left."

I love these guys.

Malik went on to earn a degree in political science. He became a bank vice-president and the youngest person ever to serve as president of the City School Board. He has run for public office and will do so again. Vote for him.

I lost track of Maurice, but I know he completed pre-calculus algebra in his senior year.

1.   Marianne and I were neighbors on the third floor of Wilson Magnet High School for more than 15 years. One afternoon I covered a class for Marianne. I was wearing a favorite outfit—black-watch-plaid pleated skirt, navy blue sweater, and white turtleneck—probably thought I looked pretty sharp. As I was expounding on the consequences of the Industrial Revolution, a young girl in the front row piped up:

"That's a Catholic skirt, isn't it?"

C.   My longtime colleague, Al, asked me to take a late afternoon geometry class so he could keep an appointment. Since I didn't teach geometry, it was a novelty. I pranced back and forth in front of the class working the proofs, firing off extra questions, and offering up little tidbits about Euclid. The time went quickly.

The bell rang and the kids filed out. A slender young man who had been sitting in the back of the room walked past me and said:

"You're not a real sub, are you?"

COUPLA KUDOS

1.   For many years, my immediate supervisor, Dana, was responsible for my annual observation/evaluation write-ups. On several occasions he told me, "You're the one who takes the skate off the steps so nobody falls."

Not something I had been aware of.

2.   In 2001, the City School District offered a teacher retirement incentive—I took it. Since nine teachers from Wilson Magnet High School took the incentive, a committee arranged one big retirement dinner for all of us. They also arranged—all very hush-hush—for each retiree to have a fellow teacher give a short speech about his/her career.

My spokesperson was Robert—a member of the Math Department twenty years my junior and one of the few African American teachers in the school.

Bob stood in front of the assembled crowd and opened with:

"Sue was a voice for the kid who had no voice."

Maybe I made a small difference, after all.

THE MILITARY

I.

I confess that I was part of the 1970s anti-military movement. I supported the removal of military recruiting from the public schools, welcomed the end of the draft, and was generally hostile toward the military establishment. Thirty years later—with my sons well beyond conscription age, of course—I feel differently.

First of all, I would require recruitment in the public schools a) Military service is a viable stepping stone to education, training, and personal discipline—for some youth, the only stepping stone. There is considerable evidence that many teens are unaware of the requirements for acceptance into the military. They take paths that preclude participating in the volunteer army and reaping its benefits. b) One could argue against public school recruitment because of the dangers of military service or the level of indoctrination or the disproportionate number of disadvantaged youth who might be put in harm's way. My position: Disadvantaged youth—rural and urban—are already in harm's way. c) I have become an advocate for patriotism. Public school recruitment would expose students to the tremendous pride that exists in the military.

II.

I have a concern about the volunteer army. Around 2005, the media reported several friendly fire and civilian-related incidents. Would a volunteer army attract/accept a higher number of psychologically marginal individuals than a conscripted army?

a) Who decides to volunteer? How many of them have exhausted other employment opportunities because of questionable behavior? I visited one of our local recruiting stations to find out what sort of psychological testing they do—essentially none!

b) A second condition that might contribute to an "instability bulge" in the ranks is periods when the army needs more volunteers. Presumably, the way to attract volunteers is to increase incentives or lower standards.

c) By all reports, the current practice of requiring multiple tours of duty is taking sound soldiers and making them crazy.

III.

Rant I wrote for a 2006 writing course:

The question is, in an All Volunteer Army do you get a disproportionate number of people who can't get jobs anywhere else—a disproportionate number of people with sub-clinical issues involving aberrations, condemnations, grandiosity, response velocity, outrage, underage? There's anger in danger; laughter in slaughter. War is hell—friendly fire is worse.

Of course, the All Volunteer Army doesn't accept everyone who volunteers. Some folks are turned down—let go to swell the ranks of the private armies engaged in private wars—self armed, self harmed, addicted, conflicted, abused, short-fused—catching children in their crossfire.

———◦◦◦———

IV.

February, 2011 : Email sent to Senator Kirsten Gillibrand

Dear Senator Gillibrand,

I am one of your constituents—a retired high school math teacher from central New York. In the past few years, I have seen newspaper articles indicating that in some army recruiting stations as many as 80% of the individuals who show up to volunteer are turned away—no high school diploma or GED, physically unfit, or have a criminal record.

Has the military ever considered sponsoring a pre-enlistment program? Something like sending potential enlistees to an underutilized base in a different state and giving them room, board, and a year of intensive academic and physical preparation. Those who successfully complete their program and, in fact, become members of the military might get a small bonus.

It seems to me such a program would meet a number of needs—not the least of which is getting some of our inner city youth on a more productive track. The one thing I'm sure of is that there is a lot of talent in that dramatically underachieving segment of our population. There is no reason why the military establishment should be cherry- picking only those who are already prepared—they could take some responsibility for that preparedness,

I have never written to one of my senators before, but I know you are concerned about creating jobs and opportunities.

Sincerely,
Sue Barocas

As of June, 2011, Senator Gillibrand has not responded. I will keep you posted.

Four Recipes Not To Be Lost
<u>My Mom's Oatmeal Chocolate Chip Cookies</u>

Cream 1 c. shortening.
Add ¾ c. brown sugar (firmly packed)
and ¾ c. granulated sugar.
Add 2 eggs, beating after each
and 1 t. hot water.
Add 1.5 c. flour, sifted with 1 t. soda and 1 t. salt.
Add 1 6 oz. package semi-sweet choc chips
and 2 c. oatmeal; mix thoroughly.
Add 1 t. vanilla and blend.
Bake at 375 degrees.

<u>My Grandmother Shaffer's Banana Bread</u>

Cream ½ c. margarine with 1 c. sugar. Add 2 eggs and a pinch of salt. Crush 4 bananas with a fork—add to previous mixture. Add 2 c. flour, 1 t. soda, and ½ c. walnuts.

Grease loaf pan. Bake at 350 degrees about 50 minutes.

<u>Best-Ever Peanut Butter Cookies</u>

1 c. shortening
2 c. sifted all-purpose flour
1 c. firmly packed brown sugar2 t. baking soda
¾ c. granulated sugar
½ t. salt
2 eggs
1 c. rolled oats (old-fashioned, uncooked)
1 c. crunchy peanut butter

Beat shortening and sugars together until creamy. Add eggs and peanut butter, beat well. Sift together flour, baking soda, and salt. Add to creamed mixture, mixing well. Stir in oats.

Chill dough. Shape dough to form 1" balls. Place on a cookie sheet. With tines of a fork, press to make crisscrosses. (Dip fork in flour to avoid sticking.) Bake at 350 degrees 8—10 minutes. (Maybe a little longer.)

Craisin-Oatmeal-Pecan-Coconut Cookies

½ c. margarine
1.5 c. uncooked old-fashioned oats
1 c. brown sugar
1 c. craisins (or raisins)
2 eggs
1 c. flaked coconut
1 t. vanilla
1 c. chopped pecans
1 t. grated orange peel
1 c. flour
½ t. baking powder
¼ c. milk

Beat margarine until creamy. Gradually add sugar. Blend in eggs, vanilla, and peel. Sift flour and baking powder. Add to creamed mixture; blend well. Blend in milk. Stir in oats, craisins, coconut, and pecans. Bake at 325 degrees 12-15 minutes, until lightly browned.

Dear V and Z—

I began to get suspicious when the Helping Hands guys in the supermarket parking lot started asking me if I needed assistance. *Assistance, indeed. Who are these chumps?* Slowly my self-image is adjusting to reality.

Here's my calculus for old age: As long as I can muster kindness and compassion for others, I have a positive presence. When my world gets so small I can think only of myself, it's time to turn out the lights. Not always a choice. We shall see.

For now, I have my new family of four, places to go, things to do. I'm a lucky woman. I still buy green bananas.

You are the proverbial wind beneath my wings. Take care of each other.

I love you,
Mom

NOTES

NOTES

NOTES

About the Author

Sue Barocas is a retired high school math teacher. In addition to her Elderwriters project, Sue is an office volunteer for Flower City Habitat for Humanity and a hospice volunteer for Lifetime Care. She lives in Rochester, New York.

CPSIA information can be obtained at www.ICGtesting.com
Printed in the USA
LVOW05s1740031113

359813LV00005B/143/P